Keep Golf Fun

By Noreen T. Chrysler, PGA

Noreen Chrysler

nchrysler@pga.com

www.keepgolffun.com

Copyright

Text copy © Noreen Chrysler, 2016

First Printing, 2016

Dedication

To thank all the different individuals, who helped with this book, would take more pages than this book already has.

I have been extremely blessed to have the support of my husband – Bill, my kids – Hailey, Nicole and Quinn, my extended family, many friends and countless golf students.

There were times when it seemed, I'd never get this project completed. Then an innocent comment or encouraging word would get me back on track again.

Thank you, to all of you, who have walked with me on this journey!

Keep Golf FUN!

Table of Contents:

From Me to You

One of the things that I like to do most in life is to teach golf. I get such a charge from seeing the excitement and gratification, on my students faces after a lesson and in the months to follow.

I believe that golf is an asset to a person's life. When I see a student enjoying themselves after a brief (or not so brief) doubt in the game or themselves, I take great pride in knowing I helped them achieve that enjoyment. Golf is such a great game and I want everyone to enjoy it as much as I do.

I know how hard an individual has to work to simply learn the game of golf. I take my role as a golf professional very seriously, it is in my DNA. When I notice someone on the course, or at the driving range who is not enjoying the game, it's hard for me not to approach them. Often I recognize a modification, either a physicality or an intellectual obstacle, which if suggested, could help the individual. It might be something as simple as standing differently.

I feel blessed to have the ability to see what aspects of the swing are causing problems and which are simply along for the ride, in order to get to the heart of any problems. I do my best to keep things as simple as possible when correcting swing flaws, even when my students repeatedly pummel me with in-depth questions about the golf swing. It is truly not brain surgery but for some reason people like to make it harder than it needs to be. Golfers, I think, feel there is a big secret to the perfect golf swing. Well, I know the secret – THERE IS NO PERFECT SWING! Happy now? There is only *your* golf swing. I strive to develop the swing that works best for the individual.

Many of my students have joked about being able to take me with them on the course in order to repeat what they had achieved during the lesson. My standard reply is that they do all the work and I simply guide and oversee. After hearing comments like this repeated many times, it occurred to me that many golfers could benefit from my collective experiences as a golf professional.

I want people who are overwhelmed by the challenges of golf to know that they are not the only ones out there struggling to learn this wonderful game. Sometimes the struggle can be with the game, their playing partners or even themselves. Often, we make this sport more complicated than it needs to be. We analyze, break down and sometimes break apart our golf swings. Often, we do this way more than we need to.

My wish for you, is to have golf inspire and energize you. The game of golf has the ability to enhance our everyday lives. I want golfers to learn to take control of their lives and to enjoy every day, through the game of golf. To do that, we need to be equipped with the right physical and mental strategies that will help us through the rough patches.

For those of you who have not had the pleasure of the game yet, I dare you to try it, even just once and see if you will allow it to enhance your life the way it has done for many others.

I have changed the names of my students to respect their privacy, but also because the names are not what is important. Their struggles and triumphs are what really are of value.

Thanks for taking the time to read this book and I hope you enjoy it as much as I enjoyed writing it!

Noreen T. Chrysler, PGA

Anyone Can Enjoy Golf

Foremost among the reasons I love the game of golf is the fact that anyone can play. No doubt my friends are tired of hearing me make that claim, but I believe it is worth repeating. Being athletic is not a prerequisite for playing golf. In fact, you don't even have to like sports! Men, women and kids of all ages and abilities can master and enjoy golf. It is as much a mental challenge as a physical challenge, and both aspects can be mastered with the right training.

Regardless of age, gender or athletic ability, golfers can fine tune their games and become accomplished players. While golf requires a degree of physical ability, mental strength is also necessary to get around the course in as few strokes as possible. The more intellectual players can "think" their way around the course, where the physically stronger players can muscle down the fairway to accomplish the same or similar goal.

As with most sports, Golf started as primarily a man's sport. Times have changed. Any golf professional who owns their own golf shop will be able to tell you that one of the largest growing markets in golf is women. We've finally figured out why our husbands are so adamant about their Saturday morning golf games – *it's fun*!

For years' women have stayed at home, stayed at the office or just stayed out of it. It's time to get in the game, ladies - literally! We have missed out on a great thing for too long. Women have many different roles these days. Some work, some stay home with kids, some do both.

When I thought of writing this part of the book I was thinking of the working person, because golf really has a great business advantage. However, one of those advantages for business can be a great source of information for others. Golf can help create new business contacts as well as being a great way to reach out to potential board members for a board you may be on or chatting about getting a new doctor. These so called "casual" conversations, can be a great source of information.

When I have professional people who are interested in learning how to play golf I try to get them to realize that playing golf is a great idea from a personal point of view and also a business one. It can open many doors. Even if your company doesn't host or attend big corporate events, the game can still be a huge business advantage to those who play the sport.

When I was an apprentice in the PGA and I began working full time, it always struck me as odd that people were able to play golf in the middle of the day, in the middle of the week. I just assumed that Monday through Friday from morning until evening, most people were at work. But if that were the case why were so many people playing golf. Were they retired? Some. Were they all independently wealthy, not likely. I found myself subtly asking people what they did for a living. Some were shift workers, some worked retail, others owned their own businesses, but many either were playing with customers or their bosses (those are the really smart ones!).

Golf and Business

Being able to play golf can be a great advantage to both men and women when it comes to developing their careers. Corporate golf outings are becoming more and more common. They are a great event for both the company and the customer or client. With the ability to write off these outings on tax returns, they are a no brainer. The golfer gets to schmooze a customer, play golf and get a tax write off. Talk about your win - win situation. Many times due to the fact that fewer women play golf, more men take advantage of this situation than women. Ladies, that needs to change if you really want to develop your career.

Golf is one of the only sports where you can truly mix business with pleasure. Conducting your business while playing golf is an extremely advantageous practice. It is in a setting that is relaxed, free from awkward silences and gives each person the ability to understand their acquaintances better.

I recently read the book "Why We Want You To Be Rich" by Donald Trump and Robert Kiyosaki. In this book, both men stated how they use golf as a business tool. Both authors talked about how they use golf to determine the integrity of a person. This is a true testament to not only the game but to its importance in the business world. A lot of business can be accomplished on the golf course. It can be a less strained setting for business deals that may be a little touchy. It allows conversations to happen more naturally than is possible in a board room. Deafening silences can mean the end of a deal at an office, but on the golf course, subtle breaks can allow for a needed change of direction.

Typically, in a meeting you have at most one hour to state your case. That meeting can be filled with tense moments staring eye to eye. Seeing who will make the first move. On the course there are 4 hours to gently slide your ideas into your customers thinking. It allows ideas to develop slowly and securely.

The longer time on the course also allows your client or customer more time to consider your position. It may also give them more time to come up with questions that are easily answered and "nipped in the bud" right away.

As well as persuading a client towards your way of thinking, it is also a great way to thank your customers and clients, creating a lasting impression and long term contacts. Taking your customers out for a round of golf will leave an impression that will last a lot longer than a simple thank you note, that will just end up in the trash. And depending on your area, it can be a great tax deduction as well.

One of my classes at school was a Sales Promotion class. In addition to lecturing at my school, the instructor ran a business selling tests to schools around the country. He had sales offices in three different states and many employees. Whenever he had to hire a new employee he would ask if they played golf. He would then take two or three potential candidates golfing. He made his decision on whether or not to hire them not only on if they played golf but *how* they played golf.

Before I go any further, the score was irrelevant. He watched how each candidate treated each other, themselves and him. He watched how they handled a bad shot as well as a good shot. How they congratulated (or didn't) each other on a good shot or consoled for a bad one.

When you are golfing, your emotions aren't just close to the surface, they are on the surface. How we treat ourselves shows a lot about what we think of ourselves. Not only did my instructor use this information on whether or not to hire someone, he then also used it to better coach and lead that individual. He could determine some of their strengths and weaknesses without even exchanging words.

Today, business deals aren't always just between client and professional it can also be between employers and employees. Sometimes employees with less experience in business, but a better golf game, get to see more places and move through the ranks more quickly – simply because they play golf. This may seem like an unfair advantage, but people hire personal and business coaches and/or read books on selling to gain advantages too. Golf can offer some of the same advantages. And, it's a lot more fun.

Many company tournaments have been put on where the non-golfers are either left at the office or worse, asked to run the tournament while everyone else is getting "in" with potential clients and customers. You are left working hard on the tournament itself instead of developing your career and having fun. How fair is that? All because you don't play golf! Now that I have you convinced to use golf as a business tool, you are probably thinking that you'll never be a scratch or low handicap golfer – absolutely not true. Knowing how to play golf does not mean shooting 73 every time you go out. It means understanding the rules, etiquette and a little course management. There is so much more to the game than just swinging the golf club. This fact is one reason why I like to spend so much time getting to know my students and why they want to play golf.

Playing golf for work can be advantageous and fun!

A few years ago I had a student Lori, come to me for golf lessons. As is customary for me, I started asking basic questions as to why she wanted to learn to play golf. It turned out, she was a lawyer and was going to be playing in a corporate tournament in about 5 weeks. The *very* limited timeframe turned out to be the good news. The bad news was that she had never even held a club before and wanted me to teach her how to play. Good thing I love a challenge.

The tournament was an event that one of her clients puts on and she would be playing with other people from this client's business but not necessarily with her client. That was also good news. We both felt that the fact she wasn't playing with her client, gave her a little out for not being the perfect golfer on the golf course. Still, we did not have much time and we had a lot of work to do.

Instead of going to the driving range, we went to my office. We needed a plan. I explained to Lori that much business was accomplished on the golf course and wondered if this was the point of the outing. Initially she felt it was just her client's way of saying thank you for all the work she had done over the past few years. However, as we sat there it occurred to her that her client had been trying to get a friend of his to also be a client of hers. In addition, she realized that this friend just happened to be who she was going to be playing with. All of a sudden her face went white. It had never dawned on her before that this would actually somehow be work. That realization changed everything.

I noticed a little bit more panic crossed her face. I assured her we could do this and we would. My challenge was to get her to be able to not just swing a golf club somewhat competently, but to chip and putt as well. Not to mention I would need to teach her all the etiquette and rules that she would need to know.

We set a plan into action. My goal was to educate this woman in the *game* of golf and to ensure that she enjoyed herself as she did it. If she didn't have fun learning the game, why bother to play it for real? We met frequently using checklists as we went.

The checklists are a visual tool I use to get my students to realize how much they have accomplished in a short period of time. It is a great way to boost their confidence when they can see, written on paper, all that has been accomplished. Far too often we look at how much we still have to do, which can be daunting. After looking at what they've already accomplished in a short period of time, students find it much easier to learn and do so, much more quickly.

In the weeks before the tournament, I equipped my student with a physical game, the right equipment, the right clothes, the right things to say, and the right places to stand. We covered the swing, etiquette, some basic rules and course management. In addition to all those things, we also spent quite a bit of time discussing the playing dynamic with other golfers. One of the last sessions that we had together we spent very little time on the driving range. Instead we were back in my office. I needed her to understand that how she treated herself and her fellow golfers might be scrutinized.

Instead of looking at it as a bad thing, I told her that this was going to be a great opportunity. She would be able to show this potential client exactly who she was and that she was a person of great integrity. Later, she told me that lesson was one of the most important and had the greatest impact on her.

So off she went to her first round of golf which just so happened to also be her first round of golf in the business world. I spent the day pacing in my office wondering how things were going. I suppose you are wondering if she played okay and got the client ... do you think I would bring it up if she didn't?

This student has developed into quite an accomplished golfer. Today she has turned the tables a little. Now, instead of the golf course being used for a client to decide if they want to use her services, she uses the course to decide if she wants to take on a new client or not. She has found it to be a very important tool in cases where she is unsure of the potential client's integrity or scruples. On a side note, she also takes current clients out on the course simply as a thank you, for their business. Some still get thank you cards, but very few – only the ones who can't golf!

So, the next time a golf outing comes up at work – go for it! Don't feel that what you shoot is all that matters. It is how you handle yourself on the course that will leave a lasting impression. In some cases, we try so hard to be professional in our careers but that professionalism can be seen as hard or cold. If associates, clients or even employees can see that you are human on the golf course, it may just work to your advantage.

When I was in the process of building my driving range I was asked by my banker to play in a charity tournament with him. I accepted, more because I love to play in charity events than because he was just about to lend me a lot of money. I had already had many meetings with him prior to this and felt it would also be fun.

We ended up playing with another banker from a different bank who had never played golf before. He said he was tired of staying at work when everyone else was out having fun. I didn't blame him. We didn't see much of him that day, as he was in the trees – a lot. Let's just say he soon became a regular student of mine, after that round.

As we played, my banker asked me a lot of questions about the business of golf. It was a great way for me to be able to show what I knew in my own surroundings. I knew all the information I had given them for my loan was correct on paper, but the golf course was a great way for me to show them first hand.

After the round the bankers both joked that they wanted only to lend money to golf pro's. That way "checking" out the business would be a lot more fun than it would be in a retail store!

Hopefully I've convinced you to somehow integrate golf into your business life. What I want to discuss next, is life after working for a living. More often these days', people transition into retirement instead stopping working completely. Some have to, and others want to. Either way as with all change, having a plan will help ensure a better transition.

Don't let golf *become* your work!

After having worked for most of our lives, the light at the end of the tunnel is retirement. For most, retirement is a welcome change of pace. It is a time when you can do what you want as opposed to what you have to do. For someone who is retired, golf relates to them very differently. We spend much of our lives working hard either at a job or at home to be able to enjoy life later on. For many lucky individuals this time of retirement will include golf.

Golf can be a great way to stay active especially later in life when your body is tired and *well used*. I say to my students all the time, "use it or lose it", meaning that if they stop moving then moving will be that much harder to do. Golf is low impact and can be played a long time in your life. Last week I had the pleasure of playing with a woman who was in her mid-70's and was just getting back to golf after having both her knees replaced. Sure, maybe she didn't hit the ball as far as she used to, or walk as quickly, but she was out playing and that's all that matters.

Retirement for many people is very different from what it was 20 or even 10 years ago. Some people have multiple interests and some even have a part time job to keep them busy and give them something to do. It used to be, when you retired you retired. You didn't work part time or (heaven forbid) not retire at all.

We are learning that continuing to challenge your brain is just as important as staying physically fit. If you came from a very demanding and challenging job, you can't expect yourself to go from full throttle to nothing. Many people play Bridge or Mahjong, some walk for exercise others work part time. Well, with golf you can accomplish both a great physical activity and a mental one all at the same time.

It is often said that golf is 90% mental and if you've played it even for a short period of time, you will agree with that statement. This is true for all golfers, but for someone who is retired the mental side of the game can take on a life of its own. Due to the fact that you don't have a job or something that takes more of your focus, golf can be all consuming. This is where retirees who work part time sometimes have an advantage. Their brain is also being challenged at work so golf is only part of their focus.

Many of my students work very hard much of their lives with the idea that once they retire they will spend most of their time on the golf course relaxing. This is a great goal but what they don't take into consideration is the role that golf plays in their lives. While someone is working, golf is a sideline distraction, something that is fun, played occasionally and put away when items at home or work demand it. Once golf becomes the main attraction, that dynamic changes.

I can't tell you how many of my students have come to me 4 – 6 months into retirement discouraged and frustrated. They assumed that if they play more golf then they will get better and consequently have more fun. Golf doesn't work that way, and neither does life. Just because you get older and have more experience in life doesn't mean that all of a sudden life becomes easy. As you navigate the different stages of your life you realize that each stage has its challenges and rewards.

Golf is the same way. It will have a different purpose in your life as the stages of your life change too. For the period of retirement, much pressure is put on the game to be a great source of enjoyment. That is great, but you also have to look at the big picture. If you think that your game will be somehow be different than before, why? What have you done differently to make it different? And, if you have been enjoying it up until this point, do you really want it to change?

That may all sound very simple, but then why don't most people follow that idea? Simply playing more golf will give you more. It won't necessarily improve your game. Have you practiced those short putts that tend to elude you right when your playing partners stop giving them to you? Have you worked on those 40 and 50 yard shots that never seem to find the pin (or the green)? I say all this because golf is such a great activity when you are retired, but often it turns into something not so fun.

My students come to me bewildered and ready to go play Bridge. I know *many* golfers don't like to practice. It's hard enough just to get them to roll a few putts on the practice putting green much less hit balls on the driving range. But, you can start to enjoy the game more without having to do too much of any of that. Use your brain instead.

Play golf with less focus and have more fun.

One particular student of mine, Carl, is the perfect example of how golf can take on a life of its own. He was about five months into retirement when he and one of my regular students came to see me. Carl had taken lessons from me occasionally over the last 10 years, but nothing very often or very seriously. When Carl retired he looked at golf with all his focus. He had been an engineer for 40 + years and now was diving into golf with the same intense focus and energy that he had put into his career. This may sound like a good idea, except sometimes that focus can backfire on you. Oh, and did I mention he was an engineer!

My student Mike, who takes lessons from me fairly regularly, brought Carl to me because he knew I could help. When Carl retired he felt golf would be a great activity to do. He signed up for golf magazines, he watched golf on TV, he even bought a few things from some infomercials. He was absorbing everything he could about the swing and equipment and even started video-taping his own swing.

None of those things by themselves are bad. Actually even together they aren't bad – unless you try and use them all at the same time! Carl was not only trying to apply all these different ideas, but he was trying to apply them to *other* people. Carl was starting to critique his buddies' games, he challenged sales people's opinions in golf retail stores but worst of all, his game was getting worse. He couldn't understand, why his swing, and consequently his game, was the worst it had ever been now that he had all this time to really work on his golf swing.

As I stood there, I realized Mike needed me to intervene more than just work on Carl's swing. He had gone overboard and was losing playing partners fast. His constant "critiquing" of his buddies was not going over well. Mike was trying to get that point across to me regardless of the fact that Carl felt I only needed to look at his swing.

Again, it's a good thing I love a challenge. Carl had spent the last 40 years analyzing, questioning and computing. He was shifting that onto golf and the people who played the game with him. So, how do you get a person who is used to over thinking everything to not think so much? Very carefully.

I don't know for sure, but I would guess that there are more books and magazine articles written on how to improve your golf swing than any other sport. Most consumers look at it as a good thing. An instructor such as myself – well, I look at it as job security. There are many great tips out there and some of them might even work for you. However, there is no one person out there that will be able to (or should even try) to apply all of them. Carl, was doing just that. I've even seen some wives cancel magazine subscriptions, because it is either that or couples' therapy.

I tend to develop a subtle tick when a student tells me the latest and greatest tip they are trying because "it sounded really good in the magazine". Every golfer is so different that in order to know what tips may work for you, you need to know a lot about what kind of golfer you are. At the very least, discuss it with some of the PGA Professionals at your local course.

As with many of my lessons, it was time for me to start digging a little deeper. I began by asking Carl about all these new streams of information. "What is it that you think all these items will do?"

He looked at me as if I was not the brightest person. "Make me a better golfer, of course," he said.

I've heard that type of statement many times. Stating "to get better at golf", really doesn't mean much. Better can be different things. Better at scoring, better at driving the ball off the tee, better at sinking more putts or just striking the ball more solidly?

The fact that Carl was being sarcastic showed me just how uncomfortable he was talking about all this. I didn't want that. I want people to understand that it is okay to need help to improve your game. I don't judge people and I certainly don't judge how they play golf. However, just like anything else, asking for help can be hard.

"All of the information that you are gathering is great, but do you realize that there is no possible way that you could or should implement all them?" I said.

He thought about that for a second and said, "But doesn't it stand to reason that more information is better?"

Ah yes, the debate of more information. I've been here many times. This is where I usually refer to using a computer. Garbage in, garbage out. Information is only useful if it is relevant to the topic at hand. In this instance, the information was about the subject but not the specific topic.

"Well, then how do I know what is relevant to me?" he asked. Great question.

"Sometimes it will be easy, like when articles are about curing a slice and you hook the ball! Others, you may have to use some common sense." I told him. Common sense is not always a word used by most golfers. As Carl, and I talked I would have guessed that he wasn't going to like the idea of thinking less as well as absorbing less, but I was wrong. He looked more relaxed and at ease than before.

"You know I've worked all my life using my brain to solve problems and fix things. I guess I just thought I had to do that with golf as well." he said. I tried to explain to Carl, that he would still need to make adjustments to his game, but that not every little detail needed to be scrutinized. Golf is more about letting things flow from you and not break them apart. "It would be nice to be able to relax a little. I guess you could say I'm not transitioning well into retirement." he admitted.

To which I responded, "Not necessarily, you just need to remember that golf is supposed to be fun, not work."

Since he seemed more at ease, I also approached the subject of "sharing" all that information with his golf buddies. Golf can be hard enough without added comments from an outside source. I reminded him that, just like too much information was crippling his game, it would do the same for his buddies and unless he was trying to make them play poorly, he needed to stop "helping".

From there, Carl and I headed to the driving range – boy was that an experience. I'm not sure how he ever pulled the club back. Just on the walk to the driving range he explained close to 10 things that he liked to work on each day. 10 things are way too many ideas and close to impossible for most people to actually accomplish. Knowing this, I wondered how much he thought during the actual swing. This prompted me to ask, "So what do you think about during your set-up?" I won't go into details, but I stopped counting swing thoughts at 15!

We discussed the importance of simplifying his thinking and allowing his body to swing the club. We were able to whittle down his thoughts to 2 ideas only. Once you learn the motion of the swing – and I don't mean perfectly, it is important to let your body go. Forcing the swing by tightening your muscles tends to make the swing worse. It took a little for him to get used to the idea, but within a few minutes he was hitting the ball beautifully.

Now, getting back to golf being a mental challenge, there is more than enough to focus on while you are playing, without concentrating on the swing itself. Direction, distance and club selection, to name only a few. If anything, most people don't focus enough on their surroundings and too much on their swings.

Carl liked to analyze things so I needed to show him that he could still analyze a lot of things on the golf course, it just shouldn't be his or anyone else's swing. I showed him how to simplify his swing thoughts while continuing to use his brain power to analyze his surroundings.

Most golfers forget to even look where they want the ball to go, much less, what's the wind doing, where on the green is the flag and so on. Focusing on where you want the ball to go is a must to play well. Players tend to look at things along the edges of the fairway that "scare" them. We need to take in all factors of the playing field, but then block them and focus on where you want the ball to go.

Play golf – if only to remember how!

Working full time can make finding time for golf a challenge. Even if you aren't working but have kids at home, it can still be a challenge. As is working part time. There are two parts to this area of life. One is when your kids are little and the other is once they get a little older and can be on their own for a bit.

When you have little kids at home that aren't in school yet, your time is truly not your own. It is a time when great things are happening in your life, but most of those great things are at home. If golf is important to you, then carving out time for you to play is also important.

When my kids were little I chose (in a not so conscious way) to have my golf game take a back seat. I simply had other things going on that at the time were more important. I didn't consciously say I don't want to play golf, but I knew I wanted to be with my kids as much as I could. As I'm learning, any parent of teenagers or older kids, will tell you that this time in your life goes very fast. At the time it seems as if you are moving at a snail's pace, but you aren't.

Today, I am playing more golf, but the great part about it, is that my kids are playing with me. They are still too young to play an entire game, but we have lots of fun even going to the driving range. A bit of a note about the driving range – my husband and I are still debating if the kids really like going to the range or if they just like getting to ride in the golf cart to get there! Either way is fine with me. They are learning a sport I hope will stay with them for the rest of their lives.

When you have kids, golf is a great sport that you can do together. It is way for you to play *with* each other and not *at* each other. You can teach your kids great things about themselves in a subtle way that they will probably be more receptive to. I think it is important for kids to be competitive within themselves as well as with others. In golf, playing against yourself is the best part. Learning how to deal with the outcome is also important. It is a fact of life that things will not always go as you plan. How you deal with that, is what building character is all about.

When I was a junior golfer, my Dad and I played a lot of golf together. He wasn't a great golfer, but he was great to play with. On some holes, my Mom and I wondered if he was still playing with us, because he was so deep in the woods. Needless to say, I wasn't that old when I starting beating him on the course. What my dad figured out quickly was that when I let my guard down about trying to beat him, I played horribly. He knew that I needed a challenge to play at my best. We came up with a game, where I would get something (usually a chocolate shake) if I beat him, but had to wash his car if I lost.

Dad knew how to ensure that I would play at my best. He and I talked a lot about the mental side of golf after that. Now, if he had brought up the mental side before I had seen it at work first hand, I don't think I would have been as receptive to it. I was one of those kids who thought my parents didn't know anything about anything. But in this case, I couldn't argue with the results.

Now that I am a parent, I realize that my Dad already knew what type of a competitive person I was. He just needed the correct platform to show me so that I would listen. On the course, is a great place to teach kids about how to handle themselves and all sorts of different situations. They are not always easy lessons to learn but better to learn them at a young age than half way through life.

Including your kids in the game, is not only great for them, but for you as well. I had put golf on the back burner when my kids were young. It wasn't something I did consciously, I just simply did not have enough hours in the day. As my kids were getting older, I noticed that I had more leisure time while they were all in school, but I wasn't playing more. I realized this was just because I hadn't made the effort to make it a priority. Trust me, it *is* now.

Even though when you have kids at home, it is a busy time of life, making time for yourself is important. Playing golf not only can be a good release of energy but a time to slow down and relax. We all get caught up in this fast paced life and forget that we have a choice of whether to stay at that pace or slow down and really enjoy things.

When your kids are little to keep yourself in the game, take your kids with you. You don't need to buy them fancy clubs, just maybe one or two individual clubs. Safety is the main concern with little kids. Make sure they understand where they are allowed to go and not allowed to go. Even ask a golf shop staff member to go over it with your kids. Sometimes it has a bigger impact coming from someone else than Mom or Dad!

Once your kids are all in school, life becomes a little different. Stay at home Mom's tend to be great about volunteering. They practically run most schools. This is all great, but, remember this is also your time. Carving out a 4-hour time slot to play can sometimes be unrealistic, so make an adjustment. Only play 9 holes or maybe just an hour at the driving range. Whatever you do – do something. Don't let it get to the point where 5 years have passed and you can't remember if you still own golf clubs!

Whether you work at home or at an office, it doesn't matter how small the effort is, do something. Figure out how much time you want or can commit and make it work. 18 holes, 9 holes, driving range, putting green, whatever it is – just do it.

Sometimes when we make the solution too big it seems unattainable, so we don't even try. If you set a goal of trying to play golf once a week, this might not be realistic. Playing a full round of golf can take at least 4 hours. On top of work and or kids, that might not be a realistic time frame.

Instead, think about hitting golf balls at the driving range once a week or even every other week. Even better take a friend. If you make a date with a friend to go to the range, you are much more likely to stick to the date. Funny how when someone else is counting on us – we get the task done. But if the task benefits only ourselves we tend to push it aside. No more pushing golf aside.

One of golf's greatest attributes is that it is for everyone. It is a mental challenge as much as a physical one, but you don't need to be athletic to play. It is a game as well as a sport but you don't need to like sports to enjoy playing golf. The young, the old, the fit and the not-so-fit, can all enjoy and play this game well.

Finding Out What *You* Want Out of Your Golf Game!

Some people might assume golf has no purpose. Some look at golf as an activity to pass the time in retirement. That is partly true. Along with being a great activity when you are retired, it also has many more ways to add to your life. The way it adds to a person's life can be as different as people are themselves. When you think about it, everything you do has a purpose. You get a drink when you are thirsty, you shield your eyes when the sun is too bright. You go for a walk when you want to get a little exercise and so on.

Some golfers, both novice and experienced, sometimes do not understand the importance of golf in their lives. They play simply because it is fun. What they don't think about, is that having fun, is a purpose.

Whenever I start a new series of lessons I like to get to know my student a little. I usually start by asking questions, about their previous golf experiences, their current physically abilities and any restrictions, as well as what their goals are for taking the lessons. I am very much a goal orientated person, and I truly believe that in golf you have to have goals to work towards.

Most of my students will look at me with a sort of bewilderment when asked why they want to take lessons, and say "uh, to get better?" That is like going to a restaurant and saying, "I'd like to have some food, please." We can work on putting, chipping, woods, irons, scoring, sand shots, punch shot, etc. The list could go on for quite a while. When I present it that way the answer gets slightly better but still not specific enough. Golfers will say they want to hit the ball farther so they can score better. While those items are related they aren't always directly related. If that were the case, then the same person who is the Long Drive champion would also be the PGA tour Champion – they're not.

At one of the courses where I worked, we had a local long drive champion as one of our assistant golf professionals. When the wind was right, he could hit the ball through the green, way past where he needed to be, on the first hole of our course. I hit the ball 220 yards off the tee, sometimes more than 100 yards shorter than our long drive champion. Guess who usually scored better when we played?

Asking students what their goals are is quite a complicated question. Mainly, because most students think that I just mean their physical golf game. To me that is only part of the equation. Why do you play golf in the first place? Is it the enjoyment of your playing partners, time away from a particular stressful home, stresses from work?

There is an assumption that if you score better you will have more fun and sometimes that does happen. However, I can remember games where I have scored well but not had as much enjoyment on the course as other times.

Think about what makes an enjoyable round of golf for you. Imagine yourself playing golf really well. Now imagine doing that, but you are alone on the golf course. Does playing well still have as much appeal? To get my kids to understand the importance of personal relationships, I use birthday parties as an example. Just before their birthday parties I ask them an important question. I ask them to imagine sitting in a room with all their friends and the most perfect birthday gifts. Then I tell them to imagine being in that same room with the perfect gift but no friends. How much fun is that gift now? Then I ask them to imagine themselves in the room with all the friends but no gifts. Which situation is more fun? For the most part they usually say it is more fun to have their friends around than any gift. (As a parent, I'd love to say they pick their friends every time – but I'd be lying!)

For many people, that is also true for golf. We find the accompaniment of our friends on the golf course much higher on our priority list than having to play well every game. Playing "well" in itself is also a relative term. I have one student who only wants to be able to hit the ball long off the tee. He and I have discussed many times that this will not necessarily help him with scoring any lower. After some discussion he agreed to not get frustrated with his scores, if I agreed to just focus on getting him to hit it longer. I knew I could help him hit the ball farther but in doing so he would sacrifice some control. In order to score well, control is important and in my books higher on the priority list than distance.

A few weeks after our lessons, he called to tell me that he had the best time of his life that day on the golf course. He was playing with his two brothers, they both scored lower than he did, but he out drove both of them on every hole. I laughed as I could feel his excitement and joy through the phone. I love getting phone calls like that. Knowing that someone is really enjoying their time on the golf course is important to me. Regardless of what they score.

Golfers who say they want to play better need to look at their games from a broad point of view. What constitutes better? Is it simply scoring better? Is it hitting more fairways or greens? Is it striking fewer putts?

For me, at this time in my life, my golf game is about enjoying the time I spend on the golf course with people I enjoy to be with. It is all about people for me. Of course I want to play well, but what the score card says is only a small part of the enjoyment factor for me. Will this change – probably. I am hoping that down the road, as my life once again changes, I will be able to devote more time to my playing abilities. But right now that time is needed more in other areas of my life. And I wouldn't have it any other way.

Many of the books I have been reading lately, talk about life being a journey and not a destination. I look at golf the same way. It is about the journey not the destination. I used to play golf with 100% of my focus on scoring. If I didn't score well, I was not happy with my game. I had rounds where I hit the ball well, but didn't score well and it would make me unhappy. Today I look at the game very differently.

I realize now what a gift golf has been in my life. After my Dad died, all I wanted was one more round of golf with him. I loved playing golf with him, as I also do with my mother. Golf changed for me when I lost my Dad, because when I looked back at all the great rounds of golf I played with him, I couldn't remember what I scored on any of them. I only remembered how much fun I had playing golf with him.

Playing with my mother is also great experience. When I was in San Diego going to school, I used to love coming home at the end of the year and playing golf with my Mom and her friends. At the time, I attended the San Diego Golf Academy, then at Rancho Santa Fe, CA. It was a school of about 150 golfers, so for most of the year I played with top notch serious players. We had fun but it was also serious golf. We all wanted to be golf professionals and knew we had to be good players to do so.

Playing with my Mom and her friends is pretty much the opposite. They laugh, they talk while you are swinging, they don't bother to putt out, and they can never seem to remember how many strokes they have taken. They are some of my most favorite people to play with! I don't think their aspirations are to become tour players but they sure do know how to have fun.

My challenge to you is to figure out what part of the game interests you the most. It may very well be the score, it might be the activity of getting out and getting some exercise, it may just be to spend 4 hours with friends. To do this, think about the birthday party scenario. If you had your best round ever who would you want to be with you? Would just one person be enough to qualify the round to others? Or is there a particular person that you would want to share the experience with?

This past Thanksgiving, the teacher of one of my children, said something that related directly to this – and we weren't even talking about golf. I had asked her plans for the holidays. "Well, we'll do a pretty traditional meal on Thanksgiving but the real fun will be the day after," she said. I was intrigued. Not having grown up in the US, I have always been surprised by the amount of focus that is put on eating and watching football on that day. I have always found it slightly odd. Anyhow, here I was in the US and someone was actually more interested in the day *after* Thanksgiving. I asked what was so fun – I should have known better. "My sister and I get to go shopping for the whole day!" Ugh. I'm not much of a shopper on a regular day, but you couldn't pay me to go shopping the day after Thanksgiving.

I had to ask what could make standing in line for hours a "fun" thing to do. "Well, we don't go to the real early sales, we head out for breakfast, then hit some shops. But if they are too crowded we just end up having an early lunch," she said with great enthusiasm.

"What is it that you are trying to buy, on the busiest shopping day of the year?" I asked with a touch of sarcasm.

"Each year is a little different. We don't actually buy that much, but we do get a little head start on our Christmas shopping. On many occasions we come home with nothing. Most often it is just an excuse for us to spend the day together and laugh." she admitted.

On the way home that day I thought a lot about what she had said. It struck me that her enthusiasm for the day really wasn't about the shopping, it was about the time spent with her sister. They both had large families and finding the time to get together was hard with all their family activities. Not to mention that when families get together completing a conversation can be difficult. My kids are at an age where there are days when I'm sure I didn't finish a complete sentence. Having time on my own to spend with friends to have some fun is cherished time. I'm lucky because many of my friends play golf, so I get to spend time with them and do something fun.

A short time ago, I received an e-mail regarding a lecture at Stanford. The professor was discussing the relationship between stress and disease. The speaker stated that one of the best things that a man could do for his health is to be married to a woman. Whereas for a woman, one of the best things she could do for her health was to nurture her relationships with her girlfriends.

This statement makes perfect sense, and can be quite visible on the golf course. The men that I teach truly are more game related and the women are experience related. The difference is that a man's take on a round of golf, being good or bad, is related to his swing and score. Women can play well, but if their experience with their playing partners is poor then the day is also considered to be poor.

When I ask students how their last game went, men almost always begin talking about their score and then move onto their swing or a particular shot that eluded them. The women will tell me how they 'felt' about the game, and then any circumstances that they believe caused a 'bad day'. They sometimes relate it back to their swing, but often the conversation ends with us discussing their surroundings.

If you've noticed in my writing, I try and use words such as usually, mostly and sometimes. The reason for this, is that we are not just talking about golf, but we are talking about people. Just as the English language has exceptions to every rule, so do people. With this in mind, much of what is written here might be the opposite for you. We are all unique, that's what makes us great.

Look at your own game. What excites you about playing golf? If you have been introduced to the game by another person, there is a chance that you have taken on their likes and dislikes about the game. Try and break away from previous ideas of the game and look at it differently. Just as in life there might be multiple aspects of the game that you find enjoyable. Think back to the games that you really enjoyed – not just your "best" rounds but ones that were fun. Think of what made it so fun. Did the score stand out or was it that it was a beautiful day and you enjoyed the scenery? Maybe you remember playing with a person, whom you ordinarily don't get to play with. It can be many different things and it only matters what you find fun!

If you've taken the time to have golf be a part of your leisure time, make sure you enjoy that time. Having a good experience doesn't always happen on its own, but you can set yourself up so that you can take advantage of all that golf has to offer.

Focus on the Positive!

Earlier this year I began noticing a trend with my students. Unfortunately, it hasn't been the most positive trend. At first I wondered if all this negativity was coming from me or was I just beginning to notice it. I went with the latter. The trend was that people seem to believe negative things about themselves more easily than positive. Now, I'm sure there are books and books written on this subject, but when you actually see it in life, it is quite, depressing. I try and only surround myself with positive people. I have a hard time relating to the Eeyore's of life. There are so many great things in life, why not choose to see those instead of all that is bad? Trust me, life's a lot more fun seeing the good than the bad.

On one particular day, I was with a student whom I had only taught for a year or so. She had called me the day before and insisted that she had to meet with me because her game had "fallen apart." I explained that the only opening I had was my lunch break the next day and if she didn't mind me chewing in her back swing, I'd take a look.

As I had anticipated, this student came about an hour before we were scheduled to meet. She began hitting balls a few spaces down from where I was teaching. On occasion I would glance over just to see how bad things really were. Well, each shot I saw looked great. All I could think of, was if she felt those were bad shots – we may be in for a bit of a communication issue.

I finished up my current lesson and felt rather invigorated to take on a new challenge. My current lesson had also come in stating how horrible things were, but by taking a look at the bigger picture we were able to see how much progress she had really made and how she was actually playing quite well. I was hoping this next lesson would be the same. (I hesitate to call this meeting a lesson, as I did eat my lunch while we talked.) As I walked closer I noticed even more good shots. Her contact with the ball looked solid, the ball flight was at a good angle and her distance seemed to be fine.

"So I see you've solved the problem on your own," I said.

"No, no, that wasn't it, wait, I'll show you," she said. With that she grabbed a handful of balls and began swinging away. Each one of these new balls did as the ones I had seen before and flew beautifully into the air. "This isn't working, this isn't what I was doing," she said. She was obviously flustered and looked very stressed. She was moving so quickly from shot to shot that I was surprised she was even making contact much less hitting the ball well. She literally jogged back to her bag to get a different club to try again. At this point I stepped in and actually took the club out of her hands. Now, I've seen some pretty upset people on the driving range – but NEVER from hitting the ball well.

"So, let it go," I told her. "Yesterday is in the past, from where I stand things look good. Your swing is better than ever." With that she insisted that all of the last 20 balls she hit *really* weren't her swing. After about four more shots she finally hit a shot that went straight sideways. "See, see that's what I've been doing *every time*." She said.

"Okay, do it again," I challenged her, knowing that the likelihood of hitting the ball that badly twice in a row was slim to none.

She hit six more balls and not one of them went sideways. "Well, anyhow, what should I do?" she asked me with total honesty. I thought for a moment. This was the trend I had been noticing. For many of my students, regardless of the amount of positive feedback they get about their games, they *choose* to look at the negative. It was becoming more and more of a stumbling block for my students and I felt this had to be addressed.

"Let me get this straight, you just hit about 30 great balls, but you don't think you can do that again?" I asked.

"Right,"

"And it took you about 30 balls to hit it badly, but you think you're going to do that every time?" I asked again.

"Right," she said again.

I had hoped that by stating how absurd her logic was out loud that she'd somehow come to her senses and realize nothing was wrong. Not so much. She continued to stand there and look at me just waiting for a new swing idea or thought that would "fix" the problem.

As adults we are taught to question *everything*. You hear statements like, *if it sounds too good to be true it probably is*, or *There's no such thing as free*. I heard someone say last week, that if we had landed a person on the moon in this day and age, no one would have believed them. They would have just assumed it was a doctored up video. Just a tad cynical in my book. I believe to ask questions is one of the greatest ways to learn. But why do we dismiss the information if it leads to us being good at something?

Here I had a woman standing in front of me who *couldn't* hit the ball badly, even when she tried, and yet was convinced that she had a bad swing and couldn't play golf. If this was the result of good shots every time, no wonder a lot of my students struggle mentally when they only hit a few good shots. This woman's thinking was an exaggerated, but good example of how many golfers think. When they hit a good shot, they are convinced they can't do it again, but seem to have all the confidence in the world that they can hit it poorly multiple times in a row.

I am fortunate that I have two parents, who not only have confidence in me, but have also tried to teach me to have confidence in myself. Having confidence from within is one of the greatest character traits a person can have. As a coach, I know that I can support and build up my players all I want, but at some point they have to learn to stand on their own.

Confidence has to come from within. Believing in your own abilities is a great gift to give yourself. We are so hard on ourselves, but occasionally we all need a break. Don't get me wrong, I continually try to challenge myself, but I also try to acknowledge when I do something right. I think for newer golfers that is a huge task. They almost always compare themselves to someone who has been playing for a long period of time.

With most of my students I set goals for a specific time period. Almost always when a student reaches that goal they just brush it off. If goal setting is a thing of the past; our society has a serious problem. Goals, once reached, need to be celebrated! We tend to forget to look how far we've come, but seem to have no problem looking at how far we still have to go. Look back at the past and feel great about how far you've come.

Can you *contact* the ball with club? – yes.

Can you get the ball in the air? – yes, wow now you're on your way.

Can you hit the ball farther than your shadow? – yes, GREAT, now you're moving in the right direction!

Can you get the ball to go in the general direction you wanted? – yes. Now you're really golfing!

These stepping stones may seem inconsequential to you, BUT at some point you had to do all of them. Maybe you were lucky and you did them all in the same day, maybe you were really lucky and you did them all in the same swing. It doesn't matter, you did them and that's all that counts.

One line I love is from the movie *The Santa Clause*. At this point in the movie the step-dad was trying to get the little boy to *understand* that Santa doesn't exist. The little boy in the movie asks his step-dad if he'd ever seen a million dollars. He said no, to which the boy responded "Well, then how do you know it really exists?" Seeing isn't believing, believe and then you will see. (For the record Santa visits our house every year – my 11-year-old figured out if you're a believer you get more gifts!!)

Well, back to my lesson. I tried to point out to Rachael, that she had dismissed the good shots and yet held on tight to the bad ones. We chatted as long as we could, but I was on a bit of a time line. We decided to meet in the clubhouse when I had finished teaching for the day. We talked at length that afternoon. After having a few hours to ponder what I had initially said, Rachel now understanding more of what I was trying to tell her.

In Rachael's case, she consistently focused on what was going wrong so much that she actually couldn't see all that was right. Some people tend to focus on what they need to change so much that they don't realize they've made the change and can move on. I can pick at least 10 things wrong with my own swing, does that mean I am a bad golfer, I don't think so. There are a lot of things that I also do well. I always try and see at least some good. I will admit that finding the good can sometimes be a challenge, but it is possible.

A few weeks ago, I went out to practice. My distance hadn't been "up to par" so I thought I'd try a few things. Well, let's just say it wasn't my best showing on the driving range. No matter what I did, I didn't get the distance that I felt my swing earned. After some time, I decided to just swing normally and see what would happen. At this point,I couldn't even get the ball to go in the right direction. Now, I'm sure to any bystanders it wasn't that bad, but compared to what I *can* do, and what I *was* doing, it was "sub-par". So, in order to practice what I preach, I thought to myself, "What good can I take away from today?"

I went through my list of things that I can usually rely on, but that day even with that list, it was hard to find something good. I finally decided that I had two things I could feel I accomplished. First, all those swing ideas that I tried to get more distance – weren't going to work. Instead of looking at it as a negative, I can now check those off and try something else. It's not a good or bad thing, it is what it is. They didn't work, end of story. I'll try something else at a later date, and I know that eventually I'll make it work when I find what works for me.

The second part, was what I call my *catch all* to keep things positive. I got A LOT of exercise that day. If nothing else my muscles had a great work out. Now, I don't know how many of you have hit a couple hundred balls when you practice, but it is tiring. And to add to it, many of which I hit with my driver as I was trying to improve my distance off the tee. I walked away knowing that I could move on with a new swing idea and that I felt great physically because I had used and exercised all my golf muscles.

So, now I have a challenge for you. The next time you do something well – **acknowledge it**! It doesn't have to be done flamboyantly. In fact, no one else has to know about it. Just you. And I don't just mean on the golf course, but in everyday life. I actually think doing it on the golf course is easier than in life. Things are pretty black and white on the course – you either hit it well, or you didn't. But don't always let that be your gage. There are holes that I scored a double bogey on that I felt proud about. Either because I kept my cool while shooting a billion, or because I saved a double and didn't make a triple.

Doing this at first will, unfortunately, not feel natural. For some reason we focus on what we didn't do right, instead of what we did. Next time you hit a tee shot and it lands in the rough don't freak out. Look at the line, is it really that bad? In some cases, you can be in the rough and actually have a better line to the pin. I'm sure the swing didn't feel good, which is why the ball went off line but look at the results not the execution.

It's okay to say you swung the club badly – because if you are in the rough – you probably did. However, what most people don't realize is that *you are upset with yourself because deep down (very deep for some) you do believe in yourself*.

Think about that for a minute. If you hit the ball into the rough off the tee, why is that bad? If you are the "hack" you like to call yourself, then that should actually be a *good* shot. However, if you actually believe that you can swing the club better and consequently hit the ball down the fairway then you DO believe you are a better

43

golfer. We hit a poor shot and we are disappointed. That disappointment comes from knowing that you can do better and that you have done better. Focus on the better.

The next time you hit a poor shot, stop and think about where you would have wanted the ball to go instead. Also think about whether or not you have the current ability to accomplish this shot. When we know we can do something and it doesn't happen, a lot of frustration comes out. Our frustrations come from our expectations not being met, but sometimes those expectations are out of whack with our actions. Circling back to Rachael, she felt that because she had reached a point where she sometimes hit the ball well, that she should do it on every swing. That is not a realistic expectation. Every shot is its own individual event. On the golf course you rarely are ever in the same place twice, nor do you use the same club on the same hole. So even though she was increasing her good shots in relationship to her bad ones, she still wasn't happy. She was basically setting herself up to be disappointed every day.

I had Rachael look back over the last four months. I knew how she hit the ball, but I needed her to see it, so for this part I tried to have her do most of the talking. That was hard to do. I tend to talk a lot! I did, however, ask lots of questions. Questions like, how far did the ball go, what direction did it fly, how did her hands feel at contact, how much thinking did she have to do just to grip the club. These were things that I knew were quite different now than when she started.

After realizing that all of those things, and more, were better, I could see her entire body relax. She had made great improvements, but had already forgotten them. She never mentally acknowledged them, so they never really stuck in her brain as great things. In her memory banks, she had focused on the bad and that was what her brain kept bringing back to her. Those memories were burned in – but she only burned in the bad. When I have students, who are in a tournament and things are not going well, I try to have them only think about great rounds or shots that they can remember. When we start playing poorly, we tend to think "Great, here I go again!" That needs to change. Bringing the good into focus not only brings your mind into a positive state, but also your body. Your body absolutely cannot perform well if it is upset and tight. If you can get it to relax you will be able to perform at a much higher level.

We need those good memories burned into our brains. Not only do they lift your spirits much better than berating yourself, but they can be used to help you play better down the road. You need to start stock piling those positive experiences and use them to your advantage.

When I was an amateur golfer, I was trying out for a spot on the British Columbia Amateur Golf Team. This particular round was one of multiple qualifying rounds that I had to play in order to qualify for the team. We were on a course on Vancouver Island that I had not played before, and didn't know much about.

On the front 9, I had an absolutely disastrous round. I shot 44, which I knew if I continued with numbers like that, there was no way I would make the team. At that point, I really felt I had blown my chances. I remember stopping between 9's and thinking that my chances were gone, BUT I really did like the course and I was playing with two players that I loved to play with. I decided that if I continued to moan and pout then my two playing partners may be affected and also lose their chances of playing on the team. I had written off my chances of making the team, but decided to wipe that from my mind and just try my best to finish the round with a positive attitude.

The second 9, I just played for fun, and enjoyed my playing partners and the course. Well, apparently I play better that way. I shot a 33 on the back and was back in the running for the team. That round, is one that I use in my memory banks when I don't play as well as I'd like. I tell myself that I've recovered before and I can do it again. Most of you hopefully don't have as dramatic a round as that, but I'm sure most can remember some round that you finished well after having the wheels fall off.

Your recollection of a good memory may be something as simple as finishing with a great putt after not even seeing the fairway on the way to the hole. Or finishing with a par or birdie on your way to shooting 100. Once you start looking, you'll be surprised at what you can find. Look for the good! Leave the bad for some other poor unsuspecting golfer.

I was fortunate in that for most of my amateur career at least one of my parents would travel with me to my tournaments. On this occasion, it was my Mom.

She would sometimes walk along the fairway with my group and sometimes wait in the clubhouse. On this day, she was in the clubhouse waiting for me. As is customary in golf, even when you are a teenager, you go in the clubhouse for a "cool drink" after your round. My Mom sat with my group and listened as we each talked about our rounds.

As my Mom and I drove back to the hotel, she kind of laughed and said, "I'm not sure why any of you want to ever play golf again." I was confused and asked what she meant. "Not one of you said you had fun. All you did was talk about all the shots you hit poorly or putts you missed or bad lies you had. Why on earth would you want to do that again?" I don't think I said anything, because she was right.

My Mom is a golfer, but she's not like most golfers, she has fun no matter what. Now don't get me wrong, she has bad rounds but never a bad day on the golf course. She and her friends laugh and giggle, but most of all, my Mom and her friends – ALWAYS have fun. I think for many of us, we choose to focus on the negative so much that we forget – THIS IS SUPPOSED TO BE FUN! As I said before, find the good and you'll have a much better game and enjoy your round more, as well as your life.

This leads me into what I want to talk about next which is 'self-talk'. Again, I'm sure there are books and books written about this. And what do they all say? *Be nice to yourself*. It's not rocket science. The key is that for most of us, we've never really given much thought to what we are thinking – yes that was as hard to type as it

47

was to read. It sounds a little odd, but it's true. Have you ever really listened to what you are saying to yourself? I would guess that even if you say something that resembles being something positive, it is said with sarcasm.

I'm not saying you have to lie, but try saying it from at least a neutral position. What I mean by that is, look at things from both ways. If you hit a ball in the lake, you could say, "You moron, what were you thinking? Might as well throw your clubs in there while you're at it!"

Or you could say "Wow, that isn't going to help my score, but at least that's it for water on this side. The next 9 holes are all clear for me." Berating yourself is like a double negative that doesn't make a positive. You've just hit a bad shot which not only didn't feel good, but will also make your score worse and now you are going to make yourself feel worse by scolding yourself. It doesn't really make sense when you think about it.

We don't like it when other people say mean or bad things about ourselves, so then why is it okay to speak meanly *to* ourselves? As I stated earlier, we sometimes get frustrated with our performance, because we know we can do better. That in itself is not a bad thing, it is actually a good thing. *The frustration itself shows that you believe in your own abilities.* If you hit a bad shot and get frustrated, you are frustrated because you know you are a better golfer – why not tell yourself <u>that</u> instead of saying you are a hack? When I have spoken about this with some of my students, they sometimes have a hard time following my thinking. In a very roundabout way, you are frustrated because you *do* believe in your own abilities.

In general, as a society, we don't promote showing that we believe in our own abilities. People are called arrogant, conceited or even egotistical. We are taught to be humble and not voice how good we are at something. We are taught that would be rude. Well, I'm here to tell you it is possible to be both, self-confident and yet … polite.

The first step with this, is to be aware of what you are saying to yourself. Most of us have this inner talk going on and aren't even aware of it. Start listening. The next step is to turn your wording around to the positive. As I stated earlier, it is okay to acknowledge that the shot was not what you wanted. In my opinion, that's kind of a fact. But, follow it up with *why* you think it was a poor shot. For example, last week I was playing and I was VERY frustrated because I hit my tee shot into the Arizona desert. Not only was I going to lose a ball (it's rattle snake season and my safety and health are worth more than a $2 golf ball!) but usually I hit the fairway every hole. I was frustrated because I am usually very accurate with my driver. When most people are pulling out a 3 wood to gain more accuracy on a narrow fairway, I'm grabbing my driver every time. It actually makes me smile when someone says, "um you might not want to hit a driver here." I look them in the eye and say, "ah, this fairway doesn't scare me." On this day last week, my frustration came from the fact that I know I am good enough to hit even a narrow fairway every time. I know for my game; I can hit my driver when I want.

I reminded myself of all the good drives that I have hit and told myself I needed to just let it go. I did, and the rest of the round went much more smoothly. Being able to stop and redirect a potential negative mental attitude is a wonderful thing!

Why else do we want to be nicer to ourselves? Not only does it make for a more pleasant playing environment, *you will also play better*! I've read a lot of motivational books and the common theme is "what you think about – you bring about!" My kids are getting a little tired of hearing that, but it's true. If you look at all the top athletes, movie stars, politicians and business people, they all have one thing in common - self-confidence. I remember watching Nancy Lopez being interviewed one day. She had been leading the tournament the entire time, but ended up not playing well on Sunday and losing the tournament. When the interviewer asked what went wrong, she simply said, "I didn't play well. It wasn't my day". She didn't rant about what a hack she was or how badly she played, she just acknowledged that she didn't strike the ball well – *that day*.

I believe that part of the equation of better self-talk is also managing expectations. What are you thinking will happen during your round today? Are you thinking you will strike the ball solidly? Do you have a specific goal in mind for what you want to shoot? Are you recovering from an injury and just want to see if you can walk all 9 holes? Part of our frustration comes from the fact that we expected a different result, essentially our expectations haven't been met. As well as speaking better to ourselves, we also need to set up realistic expectations and goals.

When I was coaching college golf, my number one player could hit the ball a long way. She was fairly confident, but was extremely hard on herself and I felt it inhibited her scoring. For three tournament rounds, when she would come in, I secretly wrote down all the words she used to describe her round and herself. I won't share the list, but in three days, she didn't say one positive thing. Not one.

At the time, I was trying to boost her up with constant praises and acknowledging the great shots that I had seen while watching her. I soon realized what I was saying had no affect what so ever. As I said before, being positive must come from with-in. I was getting to the point where I'd had enough. Her negativity. was starting to affect the whole team. Other more positive players were now coming off the course and starting to do the same thing.

When we got back from that trip, I had a team meeting after practice to discuss our up-coming travel schedule. As they arrived from the course, almost on cue, this player began listing off all the things she felt she did wrong that day. "I'm such a hack," she finally said. By now, I knew this had to stop. "Okay, well that's good to know. I'm filling out plane ticket requests, I just won't add you to the travel team." I just casually put my head down and went back to what I was doing. "What? What are you talking about? I have to go, I'm the team captain," she said.

I LOVED that she came back at me with that statement. "Well, then start acting like it," I said. She was the team captain, and the other girls definitely respected her not just as a good golfer, but as a person. In all other areas of her life she was never this negative. I decided to take this as an opportunity to talk to the entire team about having their *own* confidence in their abilities.

I told the team that each individual knows themselves better than any other person. If you think you are a hack, then why would anyone else think otherwise? We then discussed that those frustrated feelings we all get are actually due to the fact that we think we are great at golf, not a hack. If you are displeased with a shot, it is because *you think you can do better*. If that is the case, then you actually think you are a better golfer than the level you are currently performing at. All of which can be a great thing – if you approach it the right way.

From that point forward, when the girls came off the course, they had to tell me at least 3 things they did well that day.

At first, they all laughed when they had to do it, because they felt kind of awkward about it, but after a short while, they were telling me things that I could see they truly felt and believed.

As for the teams' number one player, this really changed her game; especially for her poor rounds. When you are playing well it is easy to be nice to yourself, but it is when things go poorly that it is a challenge.

The gist of all this – be nice to yourself! Start listening to your self-talk and really think about what you are saying. Confidence must come from within you. It helps when you have someone who believes in you as well, but it matters most what you think.

In addition to monitoring your thinking, check to make sure that your expectations are in line with the effort you put into accomplishing those goals. If you are the type of person who doesn't like to spend a lot of time on the driving range that's fine, but that information needs to be used when setting your expectations.

By training your brain to find the positive on the golf course, it sets the stage to do the same in your everyday life. Once you start seeing all the good around you, you will find life is a lot more fun – on and off the course.

You are not alone out there!

As I wrote this book, I let a few of my close friends know what I was doing. One asked the other day, "What is it that you want people to get from your book?" The question alone brought excitement and enthusiasm to my face because there is so much I hope you take from this book.

First and foremost, I want you to have FUN PLAYING GOLF! For many this may be a foreign concept, but it shouldn't be. I also hope that after reading this book maybe you'll see that even though you may struggle with this great game, that you're not alone out there. Many of us have been through similar situations that made us feel like we never wanted to play again, but we made it through, and for me personally, I now love the game more than ever. It has added so much to my life both professionally and personally.

There may be days when you leave the course in tears (I know I have) or you leave so mad that you feel you want to drive over your clubs as you leave the parking lot. That's okay, it doesn't mean you are a terrible golfer, it doesn't mean you should never play again. You know what it means –it means, you had a bad day. It happens. Move on. I've done some pretty stupid things in my life, but I decided in my early 20's that regret was a waste of time and extremely unproductive. So, instead, I try and learn from even my dumbest moves (and there've been some good ones!).

A bad day on the course can be the same way. If you look back on it, say, "okay, that was pretty much a complete disaster, BUT next time I can do _____ to make sure that won't happen again." I have my students use that sentence and you'd be amazed at how empowering it can make you feel. You've just finished the worse round of your life and with one little sentence you can change your entire outlook on it. I would suggest that you don't try and complete the sentence right after the round. Give yourself some time. It may be the next day, and that's okay. Just don't let a bad experience on the course be the end of a great sport in your life.

Another place I want you to feel good about, is the first tee. I can't tell you how often I've heard golfers say "Oh man, I hate the first tee!" Now, as you notice, they don't say the first hole – just the tee box. And why is that? It's because we all have this great perception that "everyone is watching me". Well, here's a news flash – their eyes may be looking in your direction, but I can say with certainty, they really don't care how you hit the ball! Sorry if that hurts your ego, but the truth is, that most people who are near the first tee are also soon going to be playing golf, and guess what is really going through their heads – it isn't what you are doing, it's what they are doing.

Beginner golfers in particular are petrified of the first tee. But as you play, you realize most people don't really care how you hit the ball- unless they are playing you for money – then they hope you miss the ball altogether!

I went down to the first tee a few weeks ago and randomly asked the people on or around the first tee what they were thinking, here's how it went: (*literally*)

"I wonder if Andy is here yet".

"I'm not sure these shoes go with my shorts".

"I haven't figured out which putter I want to use for the round".

"I'm not really sure what my tee time is. Do you know where the starter is?"

"I really hope we get done early enough for me to have a beer after the round."

"I think I should go check my bag to make sure I have enough dimes to play today's game."

These were only a few, but you get the idea. Honestly I really thought that one of these golfers would comment on the group on the tee and none of them did. I was even surprised myself. I used to joke that the great thing about some golfers is how egotistical we are. You are sadly mistaken if you think another golfer is thinking about what *you* are doing – we are only thinking about ourselves.

I will admit, though, that the first tee is just different. But then we could also argue that every tee is different for different reasons. The challenge of the first tee, is a combination of your body not really being warmed up yet and the potential number of additional people around to watch you hit the ball. I'd love to say that I now don't mind the first tee, but I'd be lying. I don't dread it, but there are still a few times a year where I feel I am more nervous than I need to be. The good news is that it's okay to be nervous. Anyone who tells you they are never nervous on the first tee, is either lying or really has low expectations of their performance. Sometimes the feeling of excitement is there instead of a nervous feeling. They are somewhat the same from an adrenaline stand point. Both elevate your energy level which is what causes some errant golf shots.

I do have one student who actually likes to be nervous. She finds it *invigorating*. We've had MANY a discussion about this and I feel that if it is "invigorating" it is probably excitement, but she still insists that she is nervous and loves it. Each to their own.

Being nervous is discussed more in the next chapter when we talk about adrenaline. Nerves are adrenaline in a way. The great news is now you know that. When you feel your anxiety level beginning to increase, take a deep breath, do some stretches or simply reassess the situation. Is it really worth the amount of anxiety you are feeling or are you making too much of it?

There are times when I know I am nervous on the tee, so I make adjustments. I know my timing will probably be altered so I make a conscious effort, for just that swing, to slow myself down a little. Adrenaline speeds the swing up, so I need to slow it down to a controlled and even tempo. I also change my focus.

Instead of wanting to crush the ball down the fairway, I focus on making good, solid, positive contact.

One last thing I want to stress, is that your golf game is for you. Enjoy each moment out there as much as you can. We get to play a wonderful sport in a beautiful setting. Much better than in a gym or a freezing hockey rink! I love both basketball and hockey, but the environment just isn't as scenic! When you start looking at the bigger picture, the stress can sometimes just go away.

Even though we play golf for ourselves, we play the game with other people. Having other people join us on our journey can be a gift or a challenge. It not only depends on the person, but on you as well. If you aren't finding your playing partners enjoyable, that is good to know, but then you need to react to that information. If it is a person you really don't care for, try not to play with them. It's that simple. You are in control of you. If you are constantly playing with someone whom you do not enjoy being with, that is partially on you. We live in a wonderful world where we get to make our own choices. Choose to enjoy your game and the people you play with.

Now, I will admit that sometimes playing with people you do not always enjoy being with, is unavoidable. You may be paired with them at your club because your handicaps are similar or they may be friends of friends. Whatever the reason, if you feel you "have" to play with this person you can still enjoy yourself as long as you approach it with the correct mind set. First, think about why it is that you don't enjoy their company. Is it something that you can just ignore for 18 holes or is it more "in your face" than that. Sometimes a simple conversation with them can help. If they are constantly talking, you could tell them that you would appreciate it if they could keep their chatter to a minimum. Or something similar. Just try and remember that you still have to spend at best 4 hours with this person, so be very careful how you word any conversations.

A few years ago, I was in my office waiting for my next student to arrive. This student has taken lessons for me for many years. Her job was such that she didn't play much in the winter, so she really wanted help making sure that she enjoyed her game when she was able to play in the summer. It was exactly time for her lesson and I hadn't noticed her car yet. This was slightly unusual but we all have days when we run late. Stacy usually came at least 30 minutes early to hit balls so that by the time I met with her, her swing was warmed up and ready to go.

A few minutes later she came walking into my office. I got up and said "ready to go?" Instead of heading towards the range, she sat down and she said, "Sorry I'm late. I want you to charge me for today's lesson, but I'm just not in the mood for golf." This was very unusual. Even though Stacy only played a few months out of the year she was very passionate about the sport and played often.

I sat back down and thought for a second. "Anything you want to talk about?"

"No," she said with hesitation, "I'm just rethinking whether I want golf in my life right now". This was an off-the-wall kind of statement coming from her. She and her husband were members at a local golf club and golf was a big part of both their lives. To not have golf "in her life", would be strange at best.

"Okay, I'll bite. What happened that would make you even begin to think of *not* having golf in your life?" I asked.

"It's not that big of a deal, I'm just not sure I want to play golf anymore." Not that big of a deal! This was a huge deal. All her friends were from golf, she and her husband spent most of their time together on the golf course and she says – it's not that big of a deal!

"Stacy, I know you. You love golf and you love playing it. What happened that would make you do a 180?" She sat looking at my office floor for a few minutes. I knew she wanted to tell me, but something was stopping her. "I just don't know if I have the same respect for the game as I did before."

One of the things I love most about golf is the high standard of ethics involved to play the game. Not all players play that way, but for over 100 years, it has been a part of the game whether we choose to play that way or not. I was trying to imagine what the "game" could have done to lose the respect of a golfer. If I was a betting person, I'd put my money on what a person had done – not the sport.

"Okay, well, what specifically happened that made you feel this way?" I asked.

Again, she thought for a moment. "Well, I was playing with the ladies group earlier in the week. And I had an experience that makes me not want to play again."

As it turned out, she had been in a situation where she had to implement one of the rules in the rule book. She went all through the process of what she needed to do and finished the hole. As she and her playing partners walked to the next tee they each stated what they had. "When I told them I had a 6, one of the ladies said that I had to add a 2 stroke penalty because I didn't implement the rule the correct way."

At this point I could almost predict what happened next. For any of you who aren't that familiar with the rules, you have a certain "grace" period of being able to fix anything that you did wrong either knowingly or not. Once you "hole" out your ball on a hole, that "grace period" is gone. Typically, it is a 2 stroke penalty for playing from a wrong place, but in certain circumstances if you are deemed to have committed a large breech, then you could be disqualified.

In Stacy's case, she felt she was right and they all agreed to ask the Head Pro when they got back to the clubhouse. The real problem, was that this was on the 7th hole and it shook Stacy's confidence. She played horribly for the rest of the round, thinking that she had done something wrong. Her integrity toward the game was very high and to potentially have her playing partners think she was trying to "cheat" was more than she could handle.

When they arrived back at the clubhouse, they went to the golf shop before settling on the final score for the round. They each told the professional their version of what had happened and it turned out that Stacy had implemented the rule perfectly and there was no penalty to be applied. Due to the fact that Stacey is curious about the rules, she asked the professional *if* she had done the rule incorrectly, and her playing partners had brought up that fact *before* they had finished the hole, would she had incurred the same penalty as if she had left the green? "No, you would have been given a chance to fix the problem as long as you hadn't "hole out".

That last bit of information was even harder to hear than her playing partners questioning her golf ethics. What this meant to Stacy was, not only did these women question her golf ethics, but they waited to do so to ensure that Stacy would have been given the penalty. If they had brought up their concerns before she had holed out, then it would have given Stacey time to fix the problem. Bringing it up after she had completed the hole changed everything. In my books – that's just not nice. There are many other words I could use, but they aren't nice either.

I could now see why her faith had been shaken. However, I needed her to see that it was *people* who she should be mad at, not the game. I had an uphill battle coming. Stacy was adamant that if this is how golf was played, she didn't want to be a part of it.

I assured her that this was about people and not golf. I can almost guarantee you that if you were to ask any Head Golf Professional if they have come across a similar situation at their club they would say yes. And the worst part – it is almost always women, not men who use such tactics.

All sports have "gamesmanship". We are lucky that golf has probably the least amount of such antics, but they can sometimes be so subtle that counteracting them can be difficult. I tried to remind Stacy of this fact, but she wasn't truly buying it.

I don't mind such antics when they are done with humor. I almost smacked a good friend of mine the other day while we were playing. I birdied the first hole, to which he replied "Oh no, looks like a case of early ripe, early rotten!' Well, I let that get in my head and shot a billion. After the round he came up to me laughing and said "I am so sorry, if I'd really thought you'd listen to me, I'd never have made that comment on the first green!" I teased him back that I wasn't going pay him the money I owed him for losing! I knew that Kevin hadn't really meant what he said, but that he was just teasing me. Truly it was my responsibility to dismiss dumb statements!

As Stacy and I talked about being mentally tougher, I told her that often I take such comments as a compliment. Yes, you read that correctly –a compliment. The way I look at it, is that if my playing opponent needs to implement antics such as verbal comments to throw my game off – they must really be scared of how well I can play!

Think about it. If they didn't care what Stacy shot, why corner her into having to potentially take additional strokes? You only need to do that if you know you can't beat the other person on ability alone. This concept perked Stacy up a little, but I kept going. I asked if she had beaten any of her playing partners. She sat for a minute to think then said, "Actually I still beat all 3". With that I laughed and couldn't help sitting there with a big smile on my face.

This was why I love teaching people like Stacy. She had just beaten all 3 of her playing partners, but because someone had questions her ethics, she had a bad day. That, to me, shows what a great person Stacy really is – she just needs to toughen up a little!

Stacy admitted that she was known as one of the better players at her club and also that it annoyed some of the ladies who played all year. Stacy played about 4 months of the year, and even in that short period of time was always pretty consistent with her game.

I then began to stress with Stacy that her game was about herself and no one else. If she stopped playing, then in essence she had allowed the antics to win. She needed to claim her own game and not let anyone dictate how she played.

We went over ways to improve her mental toughness and I had her agree to remind herself that she knows what she is doing. Sometimes players will question how to implement a rule, and that's okay. It doesn't always mean they are trying to question the ethics of the players involved, they may actually be trying to help change a situation *before* a mistake is made.

A good way to check your rules knowledge is to go to the USGA's web page and take a simple rules quiz. They give you the correct answer if you get any of them wrong, which will make it easier to learn them the right way. Finally – ask your local PGA pro if you have a question. The rules of golf are "adjusted" every 4 years and part of our job is to keep up with those adjustments. We can help you navigate the learning process to make it a lot more fun.

One final note about the rules – they are there to help you. Most people think that the rules of golf are only there to penalize you. Not true. In many cases, if you have broken a rule, they give you multiple options on how to proceed. So, in that case, by knowing the rules correctly you may have additional options that you otherwise wouldn't have known about. I could write an entire chapter about the rules, but for now, just think about them as your ally, not your enemy.

When you play golf, you play with other people. You have to consider, that if you let how they behave or play, affect your game, then you are doing yourself a disservice. Play your own game. You are worth it! Today's game is about you – no one else.

The next time you play golf, stop and look around. Look at the trees, the bushes and the grass. Look how beautiful your surroundings are. Enjoy it! Think about what a great gift this game has been in your life and how much it has added to it. Just for a few seconds, don't worry about how many stokes you've taken or what you might shoot that day. Just enjoy your surroundings and remind yourself, you get one shot at this life – enjoy it.

It's been said many times that asking for help is hard to do. Instead of asking for help sometimes we just need to realize that we aren't the only ones having that type of experience. By sharing your experiences with other golfers you will see that many of them have had some of the same struggles. You will also see that they made it through and so will you.

You NEED to practice – at least a little. Practice makes "PARfect"

I know some of you are tempted to skip this chapter, but for kicks and giggles, why not just hear what I have to say? I am lucky because I actually like to practice and I know there are many of you out there who do as well.

The good news for all of you non-practice people, is that I am very open minded. I like to include a lot of non-traditional items as practice. I feel that even taking a walk in your neighborhood is a part of practicing. It helps your health and consequently, will help your game.

So, with that in mind, let's get started. If you want your game to improve, and I think you all do, then you have to do something to make that change happen. It won't just happen on its own. Trust me, I wish it would, although then I'd be out of a great job. Putting the time in is rewarding *and* it can be fun.

The first thing I want to stress is, practicing does not need to take hours out of your day or even your week. It is the consistency and focus that matters. I would much rather see my students hitting a small bucket every few days, than hitting a large bucket or two only once a week or even every two weeks.

The more you can get to the course the better, but you don't have to spend hours there. You can change your focus each time as well. One week maybe have a goal to put your putter in your trunk and swing by the course 2 or 3 times after work and putt for 10-20 minutes. Honestly you wouldn't want to do much more than that. Your back won't like you if you do.

Then the following week, you could put your sand wedge in your car and do the same thing with bunker shots. Then, do it with your wedges, short irons, long irons and finally woods. On a side note, even if you are going to practice with your driver, take a short iron to warm up with.

You may find that you just don't enjoy certain parts of your game, but push yourself to do those anyhow. Usually, what we like the least, is what we need to work on the most. Once you put the time in practicing the shots that feel the least natural to you, you will find, you just might like it. Practice will PARfect it! You may love to hit your 7 iron, but never feel you hit your 5 iron very well, so you usually stay away from it. Take this time to practice it anyhow. On a driving range is the perfect opportunity to hit a club that you don't usually hit well. Think about it, if you hit it badly on the driving range – you aren't the one who has to go and get the ball! Make sure, however, to adjust your expectations. If it is a club you don't enjoy, it is a fact you won't hit it as well. This is not a big deal, unless you expect to hit it as well as your favorite club.

I have some students who seem to resist practicing and, I'm not sure how they expect to get better if they don't put the time in. We improve the most through repetition. If you can just get started, it is easier to keep it going. Once you commit to practicing, establish a routine. One of my students is a sales rep, so he travels quite a bit. He never travels without his putter. If he is seeing a client that lives close to a golf course, he'll take a 10-minute break and go and putt. He probably does this 3 days a week, it is now a habit and he doesn't even think about it. It is just part of his daily routine. Because of that, he and I very rarely have to work on his putting!

Try and figure out what it is about practicing that you don't like, and adjust for that. I usually practice with my iPod (although I used to use a very large Walk-Man!). The music helps me in a couple of ways, first it puts me in a good mood. I have all sorts of different music on it from AC/DC to Abba, but what the music is, doesn't matter. You just have to like it. As well as getting me in a good mood, having my head phones on helps me block out other conversations on the driving range. I love chatting with people and I have to block out what other people are saying in order to concentrate on my own game.

Having a set practice plan for each part of your game is a great way to ensure that you are practicing properly and not just spending time on the driving range. This is where working with a PGA Golf Professional can really help. I give my students not only a plan to work on, but drills on how to accomplish any changes that we want to make.

When you begin your practice session, you should always start with your short irons. Which individual club you begin with doesn't really matter as long as it isn't longer than a 7 irons. This will help ensure that you won't pull a muscle before you are warmed up.

I find that this works because golfers generally don't worry about distance with their short irons so they relax more and are less likely to try and kill the ball. It allows you to begin in a more relaxed way than grabbing one of your woods first.

Depending on what your goal is for that day, trying to use all your clubs might not be the best idea. Unless you have a lot of time, using each club won't work. I pick odds or evens. If it is an even day, then I start with my pitching wedge and then go to my 8 iron, then my 6 and so on through my woods. If it is an odd day, then I begin with my 9 and work through my clubs from there. Either way, I try and make sure that I work through every club in my bag within two or three practice sessions. Hitting 6 – 8 balls with each club is good. More is of course better, but think about how much time you have.

While you are hitting these shots, think about what it is that you are trying to accomplish – hitting it straighter or farther. Are you looking for better contact? For some, it can be something like, actually contacting each ball. I distinctly remember as a junior golfer, my goal was to get every ball airborne! I also remember the day I did it, I was so excited. I felt like I had truly become a golfer that day.

I am a big believer in swing thoughts. Our brain doesn't shut off well, that is one of the reasons we dream. So with that in mind, if we don't tell it what to think, it will come up with ideas of its own. Unfortunately, leaving our brains to decide what to think about is generally not a good idea. Take action and tell it what to do. What your brain thinks about is what your body will do.

If you can focus your mind in a positive way with what it is that you want your body to do, you are much more likely to have positive results. You may notice that I said "more likely" and not "for sure". Most people that I have taught still need to practice saying positive things to themselves – and meaning it. I know that, without a doubt, if you put your mind to something, you can achieve that goal. However, when most of us say we are going to do something, we don't always believe it ourselves. That is one of our biggest stumbling blocks.

I had a lesson a few weeks ago, where one of my students was struggling with bunker shots. Chuck could get the ball out, but it usually sailed about 40 yards past the green, much less the flag. Fortunately, we really didn't need to work that long on the shot, because once I explained that the technique was unique to a bunker he picked it up quite quickly. Within 20-30 minutes he was hitting the green every time with many of the shots landing quite close to the flag. He was confident and seemed much more relaxed.

Chuck had planned on playing after the lesson, so I walked back to the clubhouse with him to meet his group. As one of his playing partners approached, they asked if he was ready to play and did he bring his "A" game. Chuck smiled and said "Actually, I am feeling pretty good today. I should be fine as long as I don't get into any bunkers".

UGH. With that I think I actually groaned out loud! I couldn't help myself, I just stood there staring at him, shaking my head with my hands on my hips. I turned to his playing partner and said "um, fellas' I need 5 more minutes." Chuck genuinely looked confused.

"Chuck, have I taught you nothing!" I said with humor! As I've said before, most of us are taught to see our cups half empty. Mine is always half full, unless it's a margarita – then it's usually totally empty!

I tried to explain to Chuck that even if he did hit the ball in the bunker, it didn't matter. He now had the tools to get the ball out just how he wanted. In fact, he was now probably more likely to get the ball close to the flag from a bunker than from some of the places in the rough.

Instead of looking at bunkers as a problem, he needed to look at them as just another spot on the golf course. Chuck had walked away from the practice bunker telling me how good he felt about his bunker game and then not 2 minutes later stated that he hoped he didn't go in a bunker. The two statements don't go together. If he truly believed in his confidence, in how he played out of a bunker, then landing in one wouldn't matter.

When you are practicing, having confidence in the path you are taking is extremely important. You need to believe in your swing thoughts, or they simply won't work. For kids, I can give them a swing thought, and they just do it. They haven't gotten to a place yet where they question everything, so in a way, it is easier for them.

This is where working with an instructor is so important. It is also important to be able to trust what the instructor says. If you trust your instructor and know that the goal they are leading you to is where you want to go, then it is a lot easier to believe in your swing thoughts.

Some of you may ask what is a "swing thought". Well, it is an idea or a goal that we want to accomplish with that swing. With each and every student, I figure out what is most important, for that student, at that point, in their golfing career.

The golf swing is quite quick, so to tell yourself a long drawn out sentence isn't practical. You need to shrink down a swing idea, into a swing thought or more accurately – a word. For example, I have one student right now who really struggles with finishing her swing. We have gone over the importance of completing the swing and she understands it intellectually but for some reason her body fights actually doing it. In this case, we just use the word – finish. She and I have discussed beforehand what the word should mean to her. She needs to turn her hips all the way to the target, have her weight on her target side foot and be standing upright. To say all of that while swinging the club is impossible, so we shrink it down to one word – finish. As she swings the club, she thinks "finish" and what it represents.

When we are on the range we can get a little more complicated with our swing thoughts, than on the course. I tend to give more detailed swing thoughts on the range because the way I look at it we have more brainpower. When you are on the course, we have many things to think about that will affect our shot - where is the flag, how strong is the wind, what kind of a lie do I have, is there any water ahead, and so on. For that matter, I feel we should keep our *on course* swing thoughts fairly simple.

If you are asking if I think you should have two different swing thoughts for your practice session and for playing, yes – and no. I feel that even as brilliant as we all are, we can only handle about 2 ideas at a time. I can pick out about 10 things wrong with my swing – and I'm a PGA Pro. Do I work on them all at once? Absolutely not. You need to figure out what is truly important and work on those items first. Now, that being said, being on the course is much different than being on the driving range. What I like to do, so as to not have different swing thoughts at the range than at the golf course, is give most of my students 2 swing thoughts: one that will mainly focus on swing mechanics, and the other on mental focus. I don't always word it that way, but in general that is what it is.

This way you have one thought that you can have in the forefront of your mind while on the driving range, and a different thought while playing. They might seem very different, but at the same time work very well together.

Swing thoughts on the golf course should be something like, smooth, finish, or target. For some of my students it is something as simple as – breathe! You'd be amazed at the number of people who hold their breath to swing a golf club.

One item that is almost always a factor in choosing an on course thought, is adrenaline. I tend to put adrenaline in the mental side of swing thoughts, because even though it is a physical reaction it isn't tangible like your elbow or your knee. Unlike the practice range, when you are on the course, you have more on the line which will make your adrenaline go up. Even if you don't consider yourself a competitive person, you will at least be excited to be on the course and excitement translates into adrenaline.

Adrenaline can be your friend or enemy. Some people play well with a lot of adrenaline and some play horribly. A great example I like to use is John McEnroe and Pete Sampras. When McEnroe was playing, he loved to yell and scream at the referee and even sometimes people in the crowd. And why ... because that got his adrenaline going and he excelled when his adrenaline was high. Now Pete Sampras was almost the opposite. If he let bad calls or "McEnroe" antics get to him, his game started to slip. He had to play more evenly to keep his performance high. Below is a chart that many coaches use to illustrate how adrenaline affects our performance.

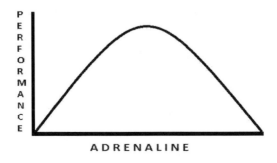

As your adrenaline increases so does your performance – to a point. If you get too much adrenaline, then your performance will decrease. The trick here, is finding out what is YOUR point. It has been my experience that most golfers tend to need a more even, low adrenaline level. I am assuming this is because golf is a long game. At best 4 hours, and it would be difficult to get your adrenaline level really high and keep it there. I'm sure you've seen many football players make a great play and turn to the crowd and beat their hands on their chest. Why are they doing this? They are trying to get themselves even more pumped up. BUT, in this case, they get to run right back on the field and go tackle someone to release the adrenaline effectively. In golf, you may run around and give all your friends a high five when you make a birdie, which will increase your adrenaline, but then you've got quite a long period of time before you are going to be teeing off again, and adrenaline has a hard time lasting that long.

This is again a place where thinking back to your good rounds will come in handy. How did you feel? Were you pretty mellow or were you pretty excited for the entire round? I have had enough rounds now that I know what level my adrenaline needs to be at in order to perform well. I can't always get it exactly right, but at least by understanding that part of the equation I can make adjustments throughout my rounds to get me back on track.

In most cases I try and use on course swing thoughts to get my students to be able to keep their adrenaline in line. This is why having a swing thought like *smooth* or even *breathe* works well. It helps keep your tempo and rhythm more even, which are the most likely things to go when your adrenaline is off balance. And without tempo or rhythm, it is awfully hard to hit a golf ball.

If you have practiced the golf swing off the course, then when you get to the course it is time to perform, not practice. You execute on the course. The goal is that you have put in enough practice time that you will be able to execute a golf swing that is consistent enough to play the way you want to. Once on the golf course, you play the way you are playing. Good or bad, that's what you've got for the day. It's like going into a final exam; you don't get to continue to study once in the classroom. You restate all that you've learned.

I once saw Arnold Palmer being interviewed. The interviewer was talking with Palmer about his routines leading up to a round. He asked Palmer what he would do if, as he warmed up before the round he couldn't stop hitting the ball right. Palmer, without hesitating, said "I'd be aiming left that day". He knew walking to the first tee was not the time to be making changes. You practice, develop your swing, then use it – as is.

There is a BIG difference between warming up and practicing. So far we've been talking about practicing, now we need to discuss warming up. Practicing is what you do off the golf course, warming up is to prepare your body to be used for the day. They are very different and have very different purposes.

When you are about to go and play, it is important to warm up. This not only will reduce the likelihood of injury, but will also have you playing at a higher level more quickly during your round. Going to the driving range before you play is – warming up – NOT practice. Your focus when you are about to go on the golf course, should be about the round, not your swing. If you have put the practice time in, then this is the time to execute what you have practiced.

When you are playing, you have enough to think about without having to "figure out" how to swing the club. This is when you want muscle memory to take over. And if you've put the practice time in, it will. While playing, you need to think about: what club to hit, how far you are, where's the flag, etc. Thinking about your swing should not be one of them. Now, don't confuse this with your swing thought. You still need to have a swing thought, but as I said before, 'on-course' swing thought needs to be simple and more general.

A proper swing thought, when actually practiced will help you reproduce a more consistent swing. It is not a new thought, and it is more about creating a positive environment than about manipulating your body's movements. This is why I say it should be a general thought and not a specific one. If you want to focus on your swing thought on the driving range while you are warming-up, that is okay. Just don't change it! Even if you don't feel that you are getting the results that you want, stay the course! The time to make changes is when you are on the driving range to practice, not to play.

Even though practicing and warming up are both done at the same place, they are very different. Think about why you are at the driving range that day. Are you there to improve your swing or to physically warm your body up for a great round?

One last thing about practice, I feel very strongly about the fact that it is important to only have one, at most two, things that you are trying to change about your swing at once. Now, having said that, for brand new golfers, (I won't say 'beginners' because it always makes me smile when a student who has been playing for five years tells me they are a beginner), you will most likely have more than that to think about. Just trying to remember how to hold the club can be a challenge much less how to get the club to swing around your body without wounding an innocent bystander.

If you really want to benefit from your practice sessions, then make sure to take it slow. When I practice I pick one idea or concept that I really want to change and just focus on that. I keep focusing on that swing change until I feel I can swing the club the way I want without having to devote too much brain power to that swing idea. Once I've accomplished that, then I've opened up enough thinking space to add in a new idea, that way, I can then begin to change.

The change may not happen with your first practice session or your second or your third, but *it will happen*. Again, this is a time when working with a golf professional can help immensely. Sometimes you don't feel you are making any progress, but having another set of eyes look at your swing can make a big difference. You would be amazed at the number of times a student of mine thinks they are doing swing A, when they are really doing swing G! It is one of the challenges of change with your golf swing because you can't see what you are doing. Often what students think they are doing in their golf swing is quite different than what they actually are.

In the 20 years that I've been teaching, I've only had one student come up to me after a lesson and tell me that they did not feel they got very much from our lesson. This student said they felt I should have given more to practice on and that what I went over they already knew. Now, ordinarily that would have upset me, because I truly want my students to feel they learned something. However, when they said they "already knew all that", I had to ask, "Then why haven't you changed any of it to improve your game?" As we chatted, I pressed a little farther, I figured if they were going to push the subject then so was I. "So, if you already know all this, walk me through what you are doing to make changes," I asked.

As the student went through how often they practiced and for how long, they started telling me what the thought process was for each shot. I am not exaggerating here – just to tell me all the things that was running through their head with EVERY shot – it took this person 92 seconds. And yes, I actually timed them. I believe it was about this point in my teaching career where I felt it was important not only for me to limit the number of swing thoughts that I give each student, but that I also needed to explained to my students why I do that.

The next question I had was how long had they'd been "working" on these things. I felt my heart sink with the answer – over a year. I knew, that if he'd broken them down in that same time period, even though it was a long list of things to accomplish that he could have completed at least most things on that list in a year. Yet, here he was with not one of the items actually completed. I hated to be the bearer of bad news, but if practiced correctly their swing should have looked much differently.

I then asked the student to trust me. It was going to be important to clear the brain of all the "stuff" that was running around in there, and really try to focus on one thing. Not ten! I have found that when I have students who have multiple things they want to work on, we write them down on a piece of paper and put it in their golf bags. One of the reasons we keep so many ideas in our heads is that we don't want to forget them – in this case, I *do* want you to forget them. At least for now. By writing them down on a piece of paper which you keep in your bag, you are telling your brain, it's okay to let those ideas go. They are in a safe place where you can read them any time you want. This allows your brain to relax, knowing that they have not been forgotten, but something else is the keeper of those thoughts now.

If you have 5 things you want to change, write them down and pick the most important one first. Your bad habits aren't going anywhere so forgetting about them for a while won't hurt. And actually, sometimes by making a really good swing change other bad habits have a way of disappearing on their own. What this means is that by focusing on one change, you can sometimes manage to rid your swing of multiple bad habits.

I was able to get this student to make a list (there were 12 items), and we discussed which would be the best to start with. The rest went into the golf bag. They agreed to give me a week of regular practice session, which was 3 times a week, and just focus on what we discussed.

Leading up to this, I explained at length the importance of narrowing focus and why it was so important. At first they weren't too keen on my plan. I explained that it was only a week and considering the amount of time already put in, what was one more week?

I am happy to report that our plan worked. The only part that was a little sad, was when the student walked back into my office. They came in and just sat there for a minute. I knew that if they actually followed the plan, their swing would improve, so I was a little nervous about how sad they looked. After a short while, they looked at me and said, "I now know why you looked so horrified when I said I'd been working on those things for a year. You were right, it worked. My swing hasn't been this good in a long time." I had wondered how this would go because I knew that if they did make the changes, they would also realize that they weren't going to get that year back – but this is where my whole 'cup is always half full' thing comes in.

The great news is that this student's swing has made a huge improvement. By clearing the brain, it made the body more relaxed and consequently allowed the student to swing the club much better. In addition to the changes that they wanted to make, some of the other items on the list either disappeared or they just didn't matter anymore. Yes, that year was gone, but due to great practice efforts, the student made bigger improvements in one week, than most people do in three weeks. Even though they were a little discouraged about the prior year, I could also see great excitement about the future.

As in most of golf, swing changes are definitely a place where less is more! The less you "focus" on the *change*, and more on already having the change – the better you will play. Once you decide on what you want to change in your swing, think about what it feels like, how the ball will fly and even what the shot will sound like. After that, let it all go. Play like the change is already a part of your game. If you focus on changing your swing, you will always be in a state of change. Focus on the completed task!

Increasing your practice time can be something as little as getting to the course a few minutes early and rolling a few putts when you would normally just walk to the first tee. If you want to get the most enjoyment out of your game, then you need to have a little discipline to move it up the list of priorities.

Play your own game

Now you don't need to be a specialist to know that men and women think differently. And, men and men think differently, as well as, women and women. But knowing is only half the battle. You have to act and live the information. Knowing this can help things both on and off the golf course.

Many of you, after reading the paragraph above are thinking, "Well, duh!" Intellectually we all understand that we think different, but we don't act like it. As your husband walks right past the big bag of garbage by the door on his way to his car – it frustrates you! He walked right past it! Didn't he see it? But reality is – he didn't THINK to take the garbage with him. Not only that, but he honestly probably didn't even see it. You, however, would have seen the garbage, taken it out and grabbed any other leaves or trash on the ground as you walked! He isn't trying to be inconsiderate, he just THINKS DIFFERENTLY. We all have different things that we find important and those things are where we spend our time and energy.

Golf is a unique sport in that it can be played by yourself. However, for the most part, we usually play with other golfers. This can make the round more enjoyable but sometimes more challenging.

On occasion, I have had students come to me ready to give up the game because they are not having fun on the golf course. To me, that just shouldn't happen. On a golf course you are in one of the most beautiful and peaceful settings in the world. Now if people don't enjoy the game simply because they don't find it challenging enough, I can handle that and will try to teach them to see the true spirit of the game. (For the record that doesn't usually happen, not challenging is NOT what most people say about golf!) But, when players say they don't enjoy their golf games because of their experience on the course I need to know why. When this happens I first like to make sure that it isn't because they are not reaching their physical goals for ball striking. Ball striking and contact are actually, in my mind, easier to adjust or fix. Which is probably why so many people practice the physical part of the game and not the mental.

Sometimes the poor experience we have on the golf course, is due to interaction with someone that we play with. This is when the real work begins. For now, I am going to concentrate on that person being a spouse. Later in the book I will go over playing golf for yourself regardless of who you play with and where. Playing with a spouse is a much more challenging process. Deep emotions are involved, and as anyone who has played golf can attest, the game can intensify your emotions without any help from other people.

My husband is also a PGA Golf Professional. This can make for some interesting games of golf. We learned early on in our relationship that it did not usually make for a good day when either of us commented on how the other was playing. It wasn't that we had negative feelings towards each other's playing ability, but just the opposite. When I play with my husband I truly want him to have a good time. I find myself holding my breath as he sets up in a bunker six feet deep to a tight pin, hoping he just gets the ball out! What I should be doing is finding my own golf ball and assessing my own lie to see how I can get the ball in the hole.

In most situations, the husband has been introduced to the sport earlier on and in so, feels that he knows more and needs to lead his fair lady down the path to successful golf. I will not dispute that he probably does know more about golf but only in how it relates to him. And as he leads his fair lady down his path it never dawns on him that she may want to walk a different path.

This is generally when the difficulties begin. As he teaches her how to hit a flop shot from two feet off the green to a pin two feet on the green (an almost impossible task for beginners), he wonders why she can't perform the shot and she wonders why she is doing the shot at all! For men, the thinking is that if their wives can hit the ball long and put it in the hole in a few strokes, they will enjoy the game. They are impressing their likes on their wives, instead of simply asking what their wife thinks is fun about the game.

For many women, they look at golf as a "two-fer". You get to challenge your body and mind through the game and chat with your friends for *FOUR HOURS*. What other sport can you say you played and at the same time got to chat with yours friends while doing it? Last time I tried to do that playing tennis I tripped over the base-line.

As women begin to play the game, husbands still hold to the idea that they have been playing longer, thus must know more and seem to have a need to enlighten their wives. Soon women find the "helpful" comments to be confusing and overwhelming. There are two things wrong with those comments. First, any of you who have taken a lesson from me will know very well that on the golf course is not the place to fix your game. You go to the driving range, make any necessary adjustments then implement them on the golf course. There are certain things that you can do when things fall apart to get you back to the club house, but none of them consist of "trying" a new thing then and there.

Second, chances are that the husband is suggesting swing ideas that have worked to fix his game. Okay, now if you are built just like your husband (I'm guessing you're not) and have been playing the same amount of time, have the same clubs, practice the same amount of time and last but not least have the same goals – then his suggestion should be just fine. Except for the fact that there are NO two swings that are the same. Swings can be similar but not the same. It doesn't matter if it is a brother, sister, aunt, uncle, mom, dad, friend, mentor or whomever – NO TWO SWINGS ARE THE SAME. There are so many character traits that make up a person, on top of our physical differences that it is simply unrealistic to think that one swing idea that worked for one person is going to work for another. It might, but the odds are against you.

In order to get your husband to be, well, less helpful, is to approach him head on. The greatest thing that you can do is to talk with your spouse to communicate to him, what you would like to get out of your golf experience. The tricky part to this is to also get your husband to understand that even if you like golf differently than him – you still like golf. For some people they have a hard time understanding that just because people think differently, that they can still get along. It's the old – agree to disagree, but in this case just agree to like it differently.

Before you do that, you need to figure out what you enjoy most about golf. Ask yourself first, what do I enjoy most about playing golf? The interesting part is that most people don't know the answer to that question. We assume that we do things in our leisure time because we enjoy doing them. That is true, but *why* do we enjoy doing them? Until you know the <u>why</u> it will be hard to ensure that you will be able to repeat the experience each time. It will also be hard to defend or stand up for yourself.

When you figure out what makes golf fun for you, it can really change your game. Some parts become less important and others more important. All of which needs to be figured out by you.

I can also tell you, this is not easy for me to do *for* a student. It would be a lot easier for me to tell them all what I think they should do. But this would be short lived. It is not a sustainable way to play golf or do anything for that matter. When you take responsibility for your actions you can be proud, that regardless of the result, you did it all on your own.

Husbands in particular have an extremely hard time letting their wives experience golf for themselves. I know I am going to get into trouble for generalizing, but this has been my experience. The part that I really like to stress with my female students is that their husbands truly want them to have a good time. *Letting* them have a good time and *making sure* they have a good time are two totally different things! But the guys don't always understand that.

To give you an example of this, I am writing this while I am currently in Kona, Hawaii on vacation. Yesterday, my husband and I had the privilege of playing a very exclusive course here, the Hualalai at the Four Seasons Resort. It was an incredible day. Even though neither of us played exceptionally well, it was an experience I will always remember. The beauty of the area was breath taking.

Now this course is not your average course, but it wasn't the complimentary food and drinks that were brought to us on the beverage cart, nor was it the bottled water they supply you within a cooler full of ice on your cart, it was the beauty of the landscape. There was lush vegetation all around, palm trees blowing in the wind and pitch black lava rock surrounding the fairways.

If you had asked my husband about that same round, his impression of the very same course was different. He also enjoyed the surrounding vegetation as I did, but he was more into the terrain of the actual golf course. We both thoroughly enjoyed the day – but in two very different ways. My husband's comments about the round afterwards included statements about his shots.

Mine were more relevant to how beautiful different holes were. Even in Hawaii my husband was focused on how he was playing despite the amazing scenery, where I was so distracted by that same scenery that I forgot about how I was playing.

This next example is a story I don't see as often but it does show how we need to give each other some space. One of my students right now is at her wits end with her husband. Keri is a soft spoken woman and is constantly being told what she is doing wrong on the golf course. All this has accomplished, is it has lead this woman to resent the game and her husband. The last time that we met she was ready to quit the game. She truly did not enjoy the sport at all. I didn't blame her after she shared with me her last golf game.

With every shot, without an exception, her husband would tell her what she did wrong and what she then needed to change. Now, Keri is a very new golfer. Taking 10-12 shots just to get to the green is not unusual. With each shot she was being told what she did wrong, what she had to do next and that she had to take a practice swing. If you think about it, she had swung the club at least 24 times and was not on the green yet. Her brain was overloaded with swing thoughts, her body was tired and her frustration and emotions were torn to shreds.

Somehow she endured nine holes of this. Then she told her husband that she wasn't going to play the back nine - which he told her was a good thing (nice!). After that comment my student wondered why in the heck she was doing all this. She was spending her "fun" time being scolded, badgered and belittled. The worst part of this was that originally her husband bought her the lessons with me because he wanted her to enjoy the game. He was right to start her with a PGA Professional, but from there he just worked against my student, and me for that matter.

I have spoken to this man on many occasions. His enthusiasm for his wife to play golf was very apparent. It was due to these conversations that I knew this could be fixed. He really wanted her to have fun. But he didn't realize that just being with him was her fun (or at least it used to be fun!). I talked with Keri for a long time. I first had to let her vent, then I needed her to realize that she did nothing wrong. She was not a bad golfer, and that she still could fix this and have a fabulous time on the golf course.

Newer golfers sometimes just assume people who have been playing golf longer, know more about golf. And, they do, but only in how golf relates to themselves. Due to all the negative comments, Kerri really thought she had no business being on the golf course. That is 100% not true. We _all_ belong on the golf course.

To resurrect the situation, I tried to bring her back to reasons why she wanted to learn golf in the first place. I truly believe in goals. It is hard to move forward if you don't know where it is that you want to go. Part of her reason to play golf was to have something for she and her husband to do together during their retirement. She also wanted to have something physical to do while spending time with friends.

Clearly, this woman wanted golf to be a part of her life for a long time. Possibly for the rest of her life. This was good news to me. Up until that point, I still hadn't been totally convinced that she was trying to play just to make her husband happy – which to me is not a good reason to play the game. After hearing her goals coming from her own mouth and in her own words, I knew we could do this. We had two challenges. The first would be changing her mind set, from not being "worthy" of being on the course, to taking ownership of her game and ability. The second challenge was to somehow *nicely* communicate to her husband that it was great that he wanted her to play golf, but that it was her golf game. Good or bad he had to start letting her discover the spirit of the game on her own.

In order to attack our first challenge, we had to dispel a few myths. The first is that you have to be fairly accomplished in your golfing ability to be on the golf course. I don't know how many times people say to me "Oh you don't want to play with me, I'm not very good". I only have two prerequisites for playing with me, that you can keep up with the group in front, and that you know how to laugh.

Speed of play is very important in golf, but it is one of those things that by making a few logical choices it is pretty easy to do. Established golfers tend to freak out new golfers by scaring them about keeping up with the group in front. Instead we should be sharing all the great ways to accomplish that goal. It can be very easy to do when you just use your head.

The only time you hear a group of golfers complain about another group is if they are either playing slowly, or not taking care of the golf course. Not fixing ball marks on the green or not replacing divots is more than a little annoying, it is simply poor course etiquette. I've yet to hear a golfer complain that someone they played with or saw on the course took too many swings (and I don't mean practice swings). Reality is if you take a lot of swings AND keep up with the group in front – it's all good.

At this point, I brought out a pad of paper and wrote down six or seven ideas on how a new golfer can play their own game and keep the appropriate amount of time on the course. As usual, my student looked at me, looked at the list and just nodded. I wrote down common sense ideas that make all the difference in the world. By showing my student how to play quickly at any ability level, it was easy to see how anyone can be on the golf course and be respected by other golfers. If you can play quickly – and yes, you can do this as a new golfer – then you can play golf with anyone.

Another myth is that you always have to keep score and play by the rules. Now, part of my job as a PGA Golf Professional, is to have my students know the rules. That does not mean I expect you to play by them – at least not at first. That may sound a little weird, but it's true. With each lesson, I try to educate my students in the physical aspects of the golf swing, but I also try to incorporate the rules of golf and some course management. Both of which are integral parts of the game. HOWEVER, when someone is learning the game, it is not always beneficial to play exactly as it is written in the rule book. That would be discouraging at best.

If a beginner golfer hits their ball under a tree, I encourage them to throw it out. Not only that, but I sometimes tell them to throw it all the way to the fairway. If you are going to cheat, you might as well do it well. Actually, I don't even really considerate it cheating. As far as I am concerned it is a part of the learning process. If that action can keep someone golfing, then I'm all for it.

Once I explain to people this idea, they tend to relax. I don't let them off the hook as far as learning the rules of golf, but I also want them to know that it can be accomplished over time. All 34 rules do not need to be memorized and executable before a person can go golfing. Some established golfers will probably agree that knowing more about etiquette on the course is actually more important.

With all that said, we started to talk about some specific tools that she could use on the course to help her feel that she was holding her own. Some of those tools weren't about actual ball striking. Most, in fact, had nothing to do with swinging a golf club. They have to do with what happens between swings and between the holes.

As it turned out, most of what was upsetting for Keri, wasn't all the swing and course information lobbed at her, it was mainly that he just didn't encourage her. All the swing "tips" and suggestions on what club to use were really not the problem. It was that she never felt, that he thought she was any good.

This realization opened up a whole other can of worms for me. I truly feel there is only one person on the golf course who needs to have any opinion on your golf game – you. Everyone else can just go throw their opinions in a lake. However, I also know that it feels a whole lot better when people that you care about thinks highly of you.

After much more discussion on self-talk, we felt we were ready to approach her husband. We set up a time and place for the three of us to meet and go over her new "goals". At the start of the meeting I made it clear to both of them that the discussion was about my student, and her opinion was what mattered – not mine or her husbands. He agreed with that, and sat patiently as she went over new goals for her game. She did a great job expressing everything in the first person, keeping with the idea that this was about her and not her husband.

As she neared the end of her stated goals, she turned to her husband and stated that he could help her accomplish these goals if he wanted. As I said earlier, he was very eager for her to learn the game, so with that he nodded quickly and was about to speak, but she cut him off quickly (but nicely). She expressed how this was her game and consequently her time to take the good with the bad on the course. She reminded him that much of what made him the golfer he was today, was the experiences that he had on the course, and that he was going to have to let her have her own experiences.

She expressed that his comments sometimes where not as helpful as he had probably intended them to be. She said that the best thing he could do was to encourage her by praising when she did something well, but to leave her to figure out the not so good shots on her own.

As I had hoped, he asked "But what if I can see what you are doing wrong and you can fix it there and then?" Great question.

Any playing partners job, is to, well, play with you. Not instruct. This line gets crossed far too often. Yes, it is easier to see the problem from the other side of the club, but it's not always the right time. Not to mention, unless you are trained in golf instruction, your experience is limited to your own game. What works for one person doesn't always work another.

Both left that day with a plan. Keri would focus on her game and her husband would do the same. This dynamic isn't specific to spouses; it can also sometimes be seen between friends. Unless your playing partner specifically asks for your help – keep your swing fundamental comments to yourself.

On many occasions I have husbands come in and purchase lessons for their wives or girlfriends. Sometimes it is because the woman wants the lessons and sometimes it is because the husband thinks she *needs* the lessons. When they come in due to the latter it is always interesting. Now, one would think that if he is going to take the step of having a Professional work with his wife, that he is on the right track – right? Wrong.

In many cases, these are the husbands that "comment" the most and can sometimes make my job more challenging. They make swing suggestions on the course, they "tweak" their wives swing at the driving range, but my personal favorite is the reviewing of all the "problems" after the round is over. These are the gentlemen that inspired my Contract for Husbands. In the contract it states that the student is MY student, that I am the Professional and unless they have more years of training than I do – they are not allowed to talk to my student about their golf games!

It goes on to say, that on the course they are allowed to give praise on good shots and that is all. If they have any questions, comments or concerns they can call me and I will discuss our goals – if the student says it is okay. I then discuss sticking with goals, and that we have a game plan that he may not be aware of – nor needs to be aware of.

The contract has two purposes, first is to protect my student from outside influences. I strongly believe that my students eventually need to be able to deflect outside influences on their own – but not right off the bat. That's what I am there for. I am a great scapegoat. When someone suggests a swing change, I have my student tell people, "I'd love, to but for now I am going to try to stick with what Noreen is having me do". That way they aren't telling people that they are crazy to try a new swing idea in the middle of a round, but rather that I have them trying something else.

The second purpose of the contract is to get the husbands to start understanding that this isn't about them. It is great that they want to support their wives, but they've got to let go. Just like having teenage drivers, at some point they have to drive on their own, and they are much better off knowing that you have confidence in them.

Usually when I present the contract, it is always done with humor and kindness. I don't want to upset anyone, but at the same time I want to try to ensure that my student will be able to get the most out of our time together. I love seeing how supportive many husbands are, and it is only a few that need a gentle reminder that their wife is perfectly capable of learning and playing this great game.

On a side note, when I was explaining the contract to one woman, I told her that it states that the husband or playing partner can only respond after a shot with "Great shot!" She then proceeded to ask if we could add in, "Can I get you a margarita?" I thought it best to leave that up to them.

If a couple can take the mechanics of the game out of their conversation, it can be a great way to spend time together. Just like for business professionals trying to win over a new client, that same "soft sell" approach can be great for husband and wives.

After saying all this, I also want to applaud the *many* husbands who support and encourage all on their own. I have many people that I play golf with, some students, some not, whose husbands are amazing on the course. They are supportive, encouraging and funny. Keep up the good work, gentlemen!

For most of these couples, they truly want golf to be something that they can do together. I have always enjoyed playing golf with my friends, but I also enjoy spending the time with my husband. Just like in a business setting, on the golf course, conversations can happen much more naturally and casually. As long as you keep swing comments out, that is.

Earlier I talked about our vacation in Hawaii. My husband and I were away to celebrate our anniversary. We decided to go without our kids (which was no small task lining up all the different people to look after them). Without the kids around to take our attention away, this would mean that we would have to ... talk to each other. For those of you who don't know my husband – and most of you won't – let's just say he is a man of few words. In recent past, if we actually had the opportunity to go out to dinner just the two of us, I would sometimes get frustrated because we seemed to just be staring at each other with nothing to say. I had these great illusions that we would talk like we did when we were dating. I always wondered what had changed. Well, our lives had changed. When we were dating, we were both PGA Assistant Professionals at the same course, we didn't have kids and very few responsibilities. We played golf just about every day, even in the off season. We played quite a bit.

Due to the fact that our lives are so busy, I feel like I have to make a list of things I need to tell or ask Bill when he gets home from work. If I don't, then it could be days before I remember to ask him again. I tell him what happened with the kids during the day, the dog and the cat, then I let him know what's going to happen tomorrow with the kids, the dog or the cat and he tells me of any upcoming trips or events that will either affect our family schedule or just his. It is what I call our time for information download. Many days we just have enough time for our "check-in's", and handling the kids before we both fall into bed exhausted, trying to sleep as fast as we can to get ready for the next day.

On this trip to Hawaii, I assumed that we would have a great time and we would "talk" a lot. Well that was only sort of what happened. We did some touristy things as well as played quite a bit of golf. It was when we were playing Hualalai that I realized for the first time why we had such a great time before we got married. It was because the majority of our time together had been on the golf course. It is an environment where conversation can just happen. It isn't forced or awkward. That environment was being recreated here in Hawaii. Now the fact that we didn't have all the stresses and responsibilities of home also helped. We laughed and joked like we did when we were still just dating.

At that point, I knew for us to grow as a couple it would be helpful for us to play more golf together. We very rarely do at home because of our schedules. However, after the experience in Hawaii I made a decision to change and play more golf together when we returned. Well at least once the weather got better – I'm a bit of a fair weather player, which is why we vacation in Hawaii!

Playing golf with your spouse can be a great experience, or it can be the most painful four hours of your life. If it isn't a great experience, have you ever stopped and wondered why? What is it that takes away from a great day? Is it that you just weren't happy with how you played? Was it that your husband/wife nit-picked at you all around the course? Or was it just simply not fun? Usually when we don't enjoy an experience it is because our expectations aren't being met. So with that in mind – what are your expectations for a fun round of golf?

Do you prefer your playing partners to be more quiet, or do you enjoy laughter and noise? Do you need them to be serious, or can they needle you a little? Every person is different and there is no right or wrong – it just is. It is what makes you happy. I know that I enjoy people who are serious about the game, but don't take themselves too seriously. If clubs are flying and swear words are every other word – to me that's just not enjoyable. One of my best rounds of golf was with three women who made me laugh so much I thought I was going to tear a stomach muscle. I had shot 2 under par and barely remembered the golf – just all the laughter. It was a great day.

With all that in mind, and once you think you know what makes people fun to play with, how can you use that information to your advantage? When you are playing, it can be something as simple as just letting each other know that you love their support but that today you'd like to relax a little and not worry about swing mechanics. I do know that many of you have great spouses that support you and your game, enough just to leave you alone, but for a few of you, this needed

101

conversation is important. If you feel that your spouse (or any playing partner for that fact) is just too involved in your game, it will be important to change that. The game you play is for you and no one else.

I love the definition of insanity – doing something over and over and expecting different results. Well, if you play golf with a certain person and don't enjoy the round, what are you doing about it to make change the experience? The way I look at it, you have a choice. You can accept things the way they are or you can make a change. If you decide to leave them the way they are, then you need to be okay with the results. If you decide to make a change, realize that your experience is about you. Meaning, don't attack other people but you can tell them you need to make a change.

For example, if your playing partner always wants to ride in the cart instead of driving but you don't want to always drive, you have a choice. You can continue to drive or you can let them know that you don't want to always drive and would they mind driving. If they say they do mind, then you can make another choice. Continue playing with this person or find someone else to play with. Once we realize we have a lot more power in our own lives, we have a lot less stress and a lot more fun.

Another area that is quite different for both men and women is competition. We are all competitive in some way shape or form. Sometimes it is with other people and sometimes it is with ourselves. Competition can be very different for both men and women. Again I am going to generalize, but this is what I see most often.

For some of you men you will find that you relate more to, is what I say about the women and vise a versa.

Many golf courses and clubs like to enhance the social aspects of their facilities by hosting small tournaments or events that involve couples. From a golf shop point of view, these events are a lot of fun to organize – and can be quite humorous. Many couples play very well together, but some just can't play golf together. When it comes to playing a golf event, even the couples that *usually* play well together can be tested.

When I say couples "can't" play together, they just haven't figured out how yet. One couple in particular really got my attention at one of these events. I'm sure there are marriage counselors out there who would have had a field day with what I am about to say. I usually try and work around the personal dynamics of a marriage, but there are a few cases where it is unavoidable.

In this particular instance, I was giving lessons to small groups of couples. I had three couples in the session. They would come out for a lesson once a week and play on the weekends. We always spent the first few minutes going over their rounds to see if their homework was working.

The first two couples were pretty much the typical couple, as far as my students go. They answered for themselves, and would only interject when the spouse was speaking to put in a word or two of encouragement or small correction. The third couple was an entirely different matter.

The husband started telling us about his round. "Well, you know I had some good shots and some bad ones." he said. He clearly didn't want to tell me his score, "I wasn't really keeping score, so I guess I'd say around 90." At this point the other two men in the group actually laughed out loud. I knew his swing well enough that he would have to play quite well to shoot that number. It wasn't really the number I was interested in anyhow. In these situations, I use the number more as a gauge than the goal.

Next was his wife to describe her round. His wife was a very nice woman, who was also very funny. She started her review with a little joke about herself. We all laughed except her husband. He just stood there for a second then, out of the blue said, "Do you really think that is funny? Who cares about your game, you certainly don't".

"Now hold on". I said. "This is Marian's time to speak, and it's about her game, so she can say whatever she wants." With that I got him to stop speaking for a minute. Marian went on to say that she felt the changes had really helped and that she was feeling better about her game. She smiled and had more confidence than in all the weeks they'd been coming to see me.

Overall each golfer, except for Terry, had felt they'd made improvements and were heading in the right direction. As we were nearing the end of our group of lessons, I wanted to make sure they kept up golfing so they wouldn't lose all their hard work. I asked each of them when they were planning on playing again. Each couple had already devised a time to play, except for Terry and his wife.

"Terry, do you have a time set aside where you and Marian can play in the near future?"

"Well, no. We've kind of decided to take a break from golf."

I was confused. Why, after taking golf lessons, you would want to not use them. "May I ask why? It just doesn't seem like the best time for a break. You've both made great improvements in your swing, so why now?"

Both Terry and Marian agreed that even though they did feel like they'd improved, playing golf just wasn't fun. That really got my attention. I started with Terry and asked what made it not fun.

"Well, I just don't feel I can play and give Marian the help she needs." He said.

Now, all the comments were starting to make sense. Terry was trying to play his own game and was "instructing" Marian as she played. Even for me, playing and instructing at the same time is hard. For most playing lessons that I do, I rarely actually play, and if I do, I'm certainly not focused on my own game.

Marian had assumed that all the "help" that Terry was giving her was normal for a new golfer. No wonder they were both miserable on the golf course. Terry had no time to focus on his own game and Marian was constantly being giving so much direction that it was impossible for her to take it all in.   Even though Terry and Marian wanted to play golf as something to do together, I needed them to understand that each of their games is their own responsibility. Good or bad. Terry had to start to just focus on himself, and Marian had to start making her own decisions on how to play.

In golf, you really have to play for yourself. You can't blame bad shots on anyone else, nor can your good shots be anything but your own hard work. I needed to find a way for Terry to feel accomplished in his own golf game without relating it to Marian's. He genuinely felt it was his responsibility to ensure that Marian did well on the golf course.

Marian, to this point in her life, had not played one single sport outside of what she had to do for PE back in school. Sports had never been a part of her life nor did she want them to be. Terry had been so excited that she wanted to golf that he was determined to "make sure" she had fun. In doing so, he made it less fun and worked against himself.

By simply having Terry focus on his own game, things improved quickly – for both their games. He learned how to play his own game and let Marian play her own game, as well. It was a different dynamic than what they had been doing, but it worked much better for them on the golf course.

Sometimes newer golfers ask for help because it's there. However, often the golfer already knows what to do, but second guesses themselves. Make your own decisions. Good or bad, you can know that you did it your way.   And that is the best way to play golf. Unfortunately, and fortunately, one of the best ways to learn about what to do on the golf course, is to just do it. You decide what you are feeling and what makes more sense to you – no one else.

One of the last items I want to talk about in regards to playing your own game, is how we approach the course, from a competitive point of view. Things in society are changing. It used to be that men were competitive and women not quite so competitive. Well, I can name a number of women I know who are quite competitive. However, we are still all competitive in a different way

In my opinion, there are two ways to be competitive – with yourself and with others. It has been my experience, that women tend to be more competitive within themselves than their playing partners, and men, with each other. For golf, we tend to be more competitive with ourselves probably due to the way golf is played. The reason why I like internal competition is because I feel it makes you a better player and person. If you are competitive with another person you are only going to reach as high as their abilities. If you normally shoot 85 and play a person who normally shoots 105, being competitive with them should be a non-issue. You should beat them without thinking about it. However, if you are competitive within yourself, every day you are being challenged to be better and do more.

Another reason I love golf so much, is that because the two types of players above – one who shoots in the 100's and another in the 80's – can be competitive with each other thanks to the handicap system. With handicaps, the player who shoots in the 80's has to give "strokes" to the other player. What this does is keep the 80's player on their toes. It is hard to push yourself from within when you know you can easily beat your opponent.

When I began coaching college golf, we were in a league in which my players dominated their opponents. We would win tournaments by 40 – 50 strokes and sometimes more. I soon found that the girls' games started to become worse. We were assured to make it to Nationals, but at Nationals we would be against players much better than we were used to playing. I had to find a way to keep my players improving their games while they played against opponents that would shoot 2-8 shots more per hole. Not an easy task. When you are playing a competitive round of golf, it is hard to keep playing well if your playing partners are *really* struggling.

I started asking my players to tell me a target score before they began their rounds for what they thought they should shoot. The score had to be based on how they were playing at the time, the difficulty of the course and the current weather conditions. It kept the players focused on where they wanted to go, as well as what they were capable of. We talked often of how to keep their focus off their playing partners and on themselves. All our tournaments at the time were stroke play, not match, so regardless of how other players were doing we needed to shoot as low a number as possible.

By focusing on a reachable target score, my players were able to put a little pressure on themselves from within. I didn't usually reprimand them if they didn't reach their target but I would sit down with them to figure out why. The purpose of the target was for them to reach their own potential.

This process worked well, and it made it a lot easier for my players to keep their games in good shape. I have always felt that being competitive within yourself is much more challenging than with another person. Being competitive with another person, instead of yourself, can set you up for unneeded disappointment. If you play with a golfer who is far better than you are, comparing your game to theirs is not only pointless but discouraging. Consequently, comparing your round to a player who typically shoots higher than you, can also have a negative effect. When you do beat them, the round tends to be dismissed as good, because you *should* beat them. That doesn't help either.

Lately, I have had the privilege of playing a fair amount of golf with a local ladies' club. It was at a course that I had not played before, and they were kind enough to inform me of where to play the ball and where to try to stay away from. The first few times I played, I struggled with the course even though, for me, it really wasn't that long or difficult. A month or so after these games, I played with the men's club and shot quite well, even though I played from a longer set of tees.

I realized that in listening to what the ladies had been telling me, I hadn't been playing my own game. When I played with the men, they just assumed, me being a golf professional, that I knew what I was doing and how to get the ball down the fairway. The men offered no unsolicited information. Because of that, I had to think more about how I played each hole. It forced me to play my own game and not how they played.

The women spoke to me from a "safe" point of view. All the information they gave me was about "staying out of trouble". Now, for the most part that is also how I play, but there are times when I know I can reach a little further in my abilities and accomplish a bigger goal.

The best thing you can do, is to think about what kind of game you like to play. Some playing partners will make club and direction suggestions. You need to decide if those suggestions are how you want to play that hole. As I said earlier, most women are more comfortable playing the "safe" route. Either way doesn't matter, except that you need to know what makes you play better.

I learned after these rounds that for about 80% of my game, I play safe, but the other 20%, I let go a little and try shots that I don't necessarily know I can execute perfectly. I find it fun to occasionally push myself, and I'm not playing for a million dollars, so why not. Think about your comfort level and how you like to play. I know it will help you play better and have more fun on the golf course.

One last aspect to cover is emotions. This is where I tend to tread lightly. Mainly because when you are talking about emotions, people get, well, emotional.

Men *have* all the same emotions women do, they just apparently don't feel like using most of them. We, as women, seem to have no problem using all sorts of emotions – and sometimes all within a 5-minute time period! I bring this up because managing your emotions on the golf course can be tricky at best.

Again, I'm going to generalize here, but just work with me. Men tend to have two, maybe three emotions on the course – they are happy, or unhappy with the occasional input of slight anger. Women, well, we are happy, unhappy, angry, sad, anxious, confused, hurt, and so on. You get the point. So in reality, men actually have it easier. They have fewer emotions to try to navigate through.

The good news is knowing all this. As I've gotten older, I've noticed that my husband and I have more "discussions" when I'm tired. When you are tired it is not a good time to have a discussion. After I have had some rest, most of what we were discussing, all of sudden didn't really matter. Funny how that works – not so funny for my poor husband though. Thinking about how you feel on the course is also very important. Feeling tired makes for a poor round for both men and women.

If you've had a particularly bad day before you get to the course, shaking it off, can sometimes be difficult, yet important if you don't want it to affect your game. Your emotions don't have to be perfect to play but you do need to be aware of them. If I'm having a day where I am feeling "off", I make sure to give myself a bit of a break for not playing perfectly, especially for the first few holes. Changing your emotions on a dime is not always easy to do or even possible. That is where you need to learn to play "with" them instead of having them work against you. Basically – give yourself a break.

Improving your experience on the golf course can sometimes be as simple as knowing who you are as a competitor. Pushing yourself to perform a task you aren't comfortable with is no better than not challenging yourself at all. Your competitive nature is with you every moment of the day regardless of whether or not you are actually playing in a competition. It is more about knowing when to push yourself past your comfort level or when to stay the course and finish strong as you are. Play golf the way you want to play.

Manage the Course Your Way

People who are newer to golf sometimes think that once you learn how to swing the golf club, then the rest of the game is easy. However, swinging the club is only the tip of the fairway! You've got all those different clubs in your bag, when do you use them? Each one has a different job and some can even do multiple jobs, so how do you know when to use them? Then there's the terrain. Some holes are up-hill, some are down. Does playing in Arizona or Colorado make a difference – Yes! In this chapter we're going to discuss how thinking smart can help lower your scores, no swing practices necessary.

Just like there are no two people alike, there are also no two golf games that are exactly alike. There may be similarities but they are still different. After learning how to swing a club, then you need to figure how *you* want to play golf. There's no right or wrong, just what works best for you. Often playing a good game of golf comes from knowing who you are as a person and what you find enjoyable. Do your surroundings intrigue you more than the equipment in your bag or do you focus more on how the swing itself feels?

On the golf course you can learn so much about yourself and the game. The key? Pay attention to the things around you, your feelings, as well as the golf swing. Use your surroundings to your advantage instead of looking at them as a problem.

Which Club to Use and When

Knowing your equipment is part of knowing your game. Every set of clubs is a little bit different because we are all a little bit different. Some sets have mostly irons and only one or two woods, some have mainly all woods and only a couple irons. Then there's wedges – most set come standard with one but as you develop your game you may see a need for a second or even a third.

Regardless of what makes up your set of clubs, you need to know how you personally will hit each club. People often ask how far a club "should" go. It goes as far as it goes. There is no set distance. A five iron struck by one golfer, could go 100 yards farther or shorter than another golfer. The distance itself isn't what is important. It is important you know how far YOU hit each club - no one else. There will always be someone out there who can hit it farther than you – get over it and move on. Use your knowledge of your game to hit higher percentage shots on the course.

Ideally, we like to see about a 5-10-yard incremental difference between clubs. Here is an example of what your distance should look like with 2 scenarios. The first one shows a 10-yard increment change and the second one a 5-yard increment change. I also put hybrids alongside which club they would take the place of.

Irons:

10-yard increments:

W - 80 yards
9 - 90 yards
8 - 100 yards
7 - 110 yards
6/hybrid - 120 yards
5/hybrid - 130 yards
4/hybrid - 140 yards
3/hybrid - 150 yards

5-yard increments:

W - 80 yards
9 - 85 yards
8 - 90 yards
7 - 95 yards
6/hybrid - 100 yards
5/hybrid - 105 yards
4/hybrid - 110 yards
3/hybrid - 115 yards

Woods:

5 - 160 yards
3 - 170 yards
1/Driver - 180 yards

Some of my student write down their clubs and approximately how far they go on a small card, laminate it and hang it on the side of their golf bag. That way they don't have to keep recalculating with each shot for what club they need. Your set may look very different than above. Most sets now only have irons as low as 4 or 5 or you may have hybrids in place of those low irons. Also some sets have sand wedges and some don't. If you don't have a sand wedge, it's not a big deal – just don't hit the ball in a bunker – problem solved.

One thing to keep in mind about your golf clubs, don't get hung up on what club you are using. For example, if someone in your group is using a 5 iron from the same distance that you are using a 5 wood, don't let that worry you. The point is to get the job done, it doesn't matter what tool you use. When you finish your round, people ask you – "What did you shoot?". They aren't going to ask you what clubs you used from every spot on the golf course. Use the club that works, not the club you think you *should* be hitting.

Terrain

Now that you know how far your clubs go – when do use each one? Just like not all golf clubs are created equal, all distances aren't either. A hole that is 300-yards uphill is going to play like 400-yards and a 300-yard hole downhill will play like 200 yards. Keeping this factor in mind helps make sure that you choose the right club for the job. 100 yards uphill could play like 120, so instead of a wedge, you may need an 8 iron. Making a small adjustment like what club you use, can make a big difference on your scorecard. As I said before, using the club that is right for the job is the important thing. Not what number is on the club head.

Things like temperature and humidity will also affect ball flight. However, unless you are travelling those things probably won't change on a daily or weekly basis. Colder temperatures (below 60 degrees) will cause the ball to fly shorter. Higher altitude with thinner air, will cause the ball to fly farther. These things might come in handy when you travel but if you are playing golf in the same area often these won't change your game that much.

Adrenaline

As well as knowing your clubs, you need to know you as well. Let's start with adrenaline. Adrenaline is basically energy. There can be good energy flowing through you, like after you just made a birdie. Or there can be negative energy, like after a double bogie or worse. Both can affect how well you swing the club. The first step is knowing, in general, do you perform better with a high level of adrenaline or a more moderate level.

If you look back to the chart about adrenaline, you'll see we all have a point where we will perform our best. Lowering or raising it, is hard to do but it is possible. I feel lowering it is easier than raising it, which is a good thing, considering most of us need to keep our adrenaline level fairly low. If you are feeling like you have to much adrenaline, take a few deep breaths and let them out slowly. Take a drink of cool water. Some people try and "work off" the adrenaline by taking extra practice swing, but sometimes this can just increase it instead. However, taking a minute to walk around a bit could help lower your adrenaline.

The interesting thing about adrenaline is that it can increase when you are happy, which most people assume means you will do better – because you are happy. Not necessarily the case. It is still added energy that needs to be handled and managed. Increased energy might not be how your body performs well. Finding that balance is important on the golf course. We need to acknowledge when we do something well. Pat yourself on the back and then reset and refocus for the next task.

Temperament

Your temperament and adrenaline are tied together but slightly different. Your temperament is more about your competitive nature. It's about how much risk you are willing to take versus the potential reward. There is a slight correlation between those who perform better at a higher adrenaline level and those that tolerate higher risk. The potential risk raises adrenaline which can be useful in the right situation. If you are standing on a long fairway with a lake in front of the green, most people would lay up. Hit a shot short of the lake down the fairway to lay up in front of the water, then hit a safe shot onto the green. But for some of us, there is that inner voice that says "Come on! You have to go for it! Laying up is boring."

The more golf you play, the easier it will be to see how much risk you perform well at. Don't ignore the result of past performances. You may *want* to be able to hit the ball to an elevated green from 200-yards out but that might not be your shot. There is nothing wrong with playing safe. However, on an occasion I do think it is fun to try shots that you wouldn't ordinarily try. If you want to try a shot that you don't usually do – go for it, BUT make sure you are ok with a potentially higher score.

Your temperament also ties into your club selection. Sometimes we feel we "should" be able to hit a ball farther than we usually do. If you are on the course (and *not* in a tournament), if you feel you should be able to hit a certain club from a certain distance – try it. From there, you can use the results to make you overall game better. If it worked, then maybe you need a little more risk to elevate your adrenaline to put you at the optimum performance level. If it didn't, then use that to make good club selection decisions going forward.

Water Holes

There are very few course out there that don't have at least one spot on the course where there is water. It could be a river, creek, lake, pond or the ocean. Regardless, it's being used for one purpose – to challenge you. It's only purpose is to make you decide how you want to play. Do you want to try and go over the water or play safe and go around?

In my opinion there are 2 types of water hazards, those that are physically in your path and those that are mentally in your path. If a golf course architect can design a hole where you can simply *see* the water, especially from the tee box, they consider that a bonus. Even if the water isn't even on that hole, it tests your brain. In this case the water hazard is a mental challenge. It isn't close to you but for some, just mere mention of a water hazard – heightens their stress, which increase – you guessed it – adrenaline.

Every water hazard will challenge you mentally and some will also test you physically. I've had some students where just the mention of water sends them into a tail spin. If you think things through, then the water isn't so scary. The first thing to do is take a good look at where the water is. In your mind, visualize that that water is actually grass – does it still hold the same importance? As I stated, some water hazards are in a place on the course that aren't physically in your way. If you are standing on a tee box and there is a small pond in front of you, for only about 20 yards – does that matter. No, it doesn't. However, visually all you can see is water. Not a great mental thought. If that 20-yard area, was grass, would you normally hit that ball there. Probably not.

When you see water, decide if it needs to be addressed because it is physically in your path or is it more of a mental challenge. If it isn't in your physical path, put blinders on and change your focus away from the water. Think of a race horse with blinders alongside of its eyes. The rider needs that horse to focus on where it wants to go, not the distractions around it. This is one reason I love to wear a hat to play golf. I use the brim of the hat to keep my eyes focused on where I want to go. I scan my surrounds to make sure I am making a good decision on club selection, then I block any negative items (water, trees, bunkers) and focus on the area of the fairway I want to go. The brim helps block distractions from around me.

120

Now, if you decide that the water is a physical challenge as well, then you have to form a game plan that works for you. If you know your driver will hit the ball too far and mostly likely go in the water – don't hit your driver. Think of each shot in percentages. How likely are you to execute the shot you want to do? If you have hit your driver over the water but not very often, then that would be a low percentage shot. If you are standing in the middle of the fairway and to hit the ball over the water is a distance you do regularly, then that would be a high percentage shot. Use your past performances as an indicator of what type of a game plan you want to do. How you play the game is not what is written on the scorecard, just how many strokes. If laying up before the water adds one more stroke, that might be a great trade, instead of a ball *in* the water that could add three.

The next time you go out and play, when you come to water, stop and listen to your thoughts. Does the water stress you? If so, why. Is it really a problem or is it just put there to distract you? If it is physically between you and the putting green, make a plan. What is the best way to work around – or over it? It is just another situation on the golf course, that needs to be dealt with.

Taking charge of your thoughts is imperative when it comes to challenging situations on the golf course. Work with your thoughts instead of trying to fight them. It's okay to say this is a tough hole, but them make a plan to conquer it.

I'm a big believer in giving yourself a break, just be careful that you aren't in a roundabout way telling yourself that you don't believe in your abilities. A few weeks back I was playing with a student. We came to a par three where there was a small pond in front of the tee box. It was a short hole and I knew this player could easier clear the water all the way to the green.

When we approached the tee box, I noticed she went into her bag and took out a different ball. I was curious what prompted the change, so I asked.

"Well, I switched to an old ball. That way if it goes in the water it won't matter."

I think I visibly gave my head a shake.

"So, let me get this straight. You are okay with going in the water?"

"No. I just don't want to lose a good ball; in case I do."

By changing to an "old" ball, she wasn't invested in making sure she executed the shot well. She might as well have thrown the ball and see how far it went. By changing balls, she was telling herself it was okay to do poorly. That is not the message you want to give yourself.

I had her visualize the pond as grass and showed her that this water was only a mental hazard, and she was giving into it. Also, I had her change back to her original ball. In doing so, this commits the golfer to the shot. It is a good way to prove to yourself that you have the confidence to do the shot that you need to do. This is an example of where temperament comes in. In this case the student was trying to reduce the amount of pressure on her self – good, but in doing it this way, she was sending the wrong message to her mind – bad.

In this example, if she really didn't have the physical game to get over the water, then changing balls might have been a good thing, although I still don't suggest it. Try the shot, if it doesn't work, it's only a golf ball. Possibly a great investment into your golf future!

Putting vs chipping

This next situation won't happen every hole and may not happen every round. If your ball lands on the fringe (aka, skirt, apron, second cut, etc.), do you putt the ball or chip it? The answer is, yes. You can do either. Here is the important part, whichever you decide to do, only do it if you have practiced it.

Some people feel more comfortable with their putters in their hands so even if the ball is off the green and on the fridge, then they want to putt it. That's great, but have you done it before? The speed at which the ball is going to roll on the putting green is different than on the fringe. Adjusting for that is important. Instead of having one speed to contend with, you'll have two different speeds in one putt. That can be challenging for some.

Some players prefer a wedge in their hands if the grass is anything thicker than the putting green. Again, that's great. But have you practice really short wedge shots from just off the green? This is a situation where having touch over power is important.

In some instances, the decision will be made for you. If there are irregularities in the grass between you and the flag, chipping will be a better choice, as you can carry the ball over the problem. If the grass is in good shape, then you get to decide which club will work best for you. Even if you have practiced both, listening to yourself is still the most important factor for choosing which club. Take both clubs to the spot where your ball is, stand looking at the shot with your wedge in your hand. Then switch clubs and do the same thing. Which one *feels* better. As you learn to listen to your feelings and body more, the decision will be much easier. You'll know which club to use by how you feel.

Know Your Environment and Yourself

Knowing how to swing a golf club is a wonderful start to the game of golf. Then, when you get on the golf course, what do you do with that wonderful golf swing? Along with how to swing the club, you need to know when to use which club. In order to figure that part of the equation out, you need to know your surroundings. Things like the weather can affect ball flight which may affect your club selection choice. Other things like the terrain can also affect your club choice. Terrain won't just include if you are uphill or down. It also includes how level your stance is, which can affect your balance. It will also include the length of grass. Are you in the rough or the fairway? Longer grass can make contact more challenging which again, may change your decision when it comes to club selection.

Learning many of these details comes with time and experience. The kicker about experience, is that it is your experience. Not someone else's. A coach or a friend can tell you different ways to approach each shot but you have to ultimately decide what *you* want to do. Often when we hit a shot poorly or it doesn't go where we want it to, we assume we hit the shot wrong. That may not be the case, it could be that it was the wrong shot to hit. Maybe you were trying to hit a 3 iron out of the rough. Is that a possible shot? Sure. But that might not be the shot that works the best for you. You might be more comfortable with shorter iron, which might not get you all the way to the green, but will most definitely get you out of the long grass.

We often talk in golf about playing smart. Some think that playing smart means playing safe, and often it is but not always. Playing smart is really just playing your own game. You sometimes have to listen to that inner feeling that is telling you to try and "go for it". If you constantly hold back, then you'll never really know what you are capable of. Just make sure to pick the right time. While playing in a competitive round, that isn't the time to try something new. During a regular round of golf can be a great time to push yourself a little more. If you decide to do this, remind yourself that the benefit is in learning a little more about you and your game – not a low score. Both are important.

When it comes to knowing ourselves, we need to start being a better listener. Anxiety, nervousness, angst

– these are all signs that your body is trying to tell you something. There are always going to be first tee jitters. That is a little different than what I'm thinking about.

First tee jitters are what they are. You learn to work with them. Here are few things you can do to help make that first tee more fun:

- Take a few deep breaths.
- Remind yourself that all those people "looking" at you, are really focused on themselves.
- Focus on a smooth swing, as opposed to blasting it down the fairway. Give your body time be in "golf" mode.

Once you are a little deeper into your round, that same jittery, nervous feeling can be trying to tell you something else. If you are trying to decide between clubs it might be telling you, you haven't chosen the correct club. It can also be telling you that mentally you aren't committed to the shot.

To figure out the best way to settle down, start with your feelings. Stand, as I suggested on the putting green, behind the shot with different clubs in your hand and see if you can *feel* which club is the right choice. It could be a subtle change in how you feel, so you really have to listen. Does your posture change? Do you feel more confident with one over the other? Again, listening to your body and your feelings make a big difference.

If neither club is improving your confidence, then we turn to logic as an additional factor. Look at the shot.

Really look at it. What is the distance? What is your lie like? How are you feeling – strong, tired, off? As you answer each of these questions, it will become a logical choice for which club to use. If you are feeling a little tired, the club with more distance is probably a better choice. Sometimes we need to walk through the process of what we need to do, to execute a good shot in order to get the confidence we need, to do just that.

Speed of Play

One of the most talked about aspects of golf, is Speed of Play. More specifically how quickly – or not, a player plays a round of golf. When people find out I'm a PGA golf professional, they quickly say that I wouldn't want to play with them because they aren't very good. The truth is, I really don't care *how* a person plays, only that they have good etiquette – and that includes speed of play.

And, what does speed of play mean, playing golf – in a timely manner – not quickly. There are many things that golfers can do between shots that help them play faster. First, is being ready. We all like to chat on the golf course, but you have to make sure that your chatting isn't at the sake of knowing when it is your turn to hit the golf ball.

Being ready doesn't just mean being at your ball when it is your turn. You should have your club in your hand and ready to swing by the time it is your turn. Your focus should start to turn to your next shot before you even arrive at your ball. As you are approaching the shot, you can be determining how far you are which will help narrow down which club you need to use. As you reach your ball, you can add what type of lie you have to the equation to help decide which club to use. From there, once it is your turn, take one practice swing, then hit the ball.

As I've said, practice swings on the course are about settling you down, not improving your golf game. They have a different goal than when you are actually practicing on the driving range. If you are feeling really unsettled about the shot, stepping away and taking a deep breath will do more good than an additional practice swing.

Other things you can do to play quickly are to write down your score on the next tee box – not the putting green. As others are teeing off in your group, that is the perfect time to write down scores, not while golfers behind you are waiting to hit onto the green.

If you need to take a wedge with you, as well as a putter, onto the green, once you have finished with the wedge, make sure to place it between your bag and the flag stick. After you put your ball in the hole and are heading back to your bag, if your club is lying so you will literally step on it, then you will not forget it, and you won't take additional time to go and retrieve it.

The next idea may seem backwards but is one of the best ways to play in a timely manner. Swing slowly! Yes, I'm talking about playing fast and I just said swing slowly. Moving between shots and being ready to hit the ball are good times to do things quickly. While actually swinging the club, is not. If you rush your swing, you will most likely hit the ball poorly resulting in a potential additional golf shot.

Let's break this down. Let's say it takes up to 2 minutes to get to your ball and hit it. If you take an extra 20 seconds to stop and take a deep breath to settle yourself down, you are much more likely to hit the ball well. However, if you rush the shot and end up hitting it poorly, and you have to take *another* shot, then you've added another 2 minutes to your time. 20 seconds is a lot less time than 2 minutes. Add that up a few times a hole and it can make a big difference in your round.

New golfers sometimes get a bad rep as being slow. I find that new golfers want to know the right way to play and thus tend to play more quickly than most. It's the more established golfers that tend to take themselves or the game too seriously that slow the course down. Remember that it's a game and meant to be enjoyed – by everyone.

If you are a newer golfer – **be okay with picking up the ball**. Once you have taken a certain amount of strokes, pick the ball up and put it on the green. This one sometimes seems "anti" golf but it is necessary sometimes to keep things moving. And how do you determine how many strokes to take before you pick the ball up? Well, the easiest way is to use the par of the hole. "Par" is based on a "scratch" golfer (i.e. a very good player) – not you. However, you can use it to help you know when to pick the ball up. Once you are at double the par – 6 on a par 3, 8 on a par 4, 10 on a par 5, pick the ball up. Place the ball on the green and putt from there. By the way 10 shots is a lot, you may want your maximum number of strokes to not exceed 8!

The next time you are out on the golf course, use your mind as well as your body to help improve your game. Think about what it is you want to happen on each and every shot. When your body and mind work together you can perform at a much higher level.

By thinking about all your surrounds while you play, you manage your game as a whole and not just how to swing the club. There's a lot more to putting the ball in the hole at the end of the fairway than just swinging the golf club.

Golf Links Life

Golf is a sport that you enjoy in a beautiful setting, with friends or family at your side. If you take a minute the next time you play, and just stop and look around, you will see the many wonderful experiences golf can bring you. Sometimes we forget to stop and "smell the roses" and we don't see how great the big picture of life is.

Often we let little things distract us from how great life really is. Golf is played in some of the most beautiful places in the world. Enjoy that part of the game as well as the game itself. Often we need that part of the game to help with things going on and off the golf course. The game and its' surrounds can be therapeutic, if you let them.

When Shelley first came to me, she was slightly apprehensive and seemed distracted. A friend had given her the lessons as a gift. In cases like this, it is meant with good intentions, but not always the gift the person wants. I wondered if that were the case here. I asked a few questions and she genuinely seemed to be interested in learning the game so we proceeded with the lesson.

Things went very well that first day. She improved quickly and we ended up having quite a few laughs along the way. Shelley had been on the course once before so she knew enough that we were able to make a good amount of progress. We were scheduled to meet for six weeks, so I gave her homework and told her I'd see her in a week.

When she returned the following week, she had admitted that she had originally only taken the golf lessons to keep her husband and friend happy. He had been encouraging her to play the game and when her friend bought the lessons she felt it would be less effort just to do the lessons than argue with him. However, after showing her that you can actually laugh *and* play golf, she began to love the game.

In addition to our weekly meeting, I had asked Shelley to work into her schedule a time to practice at least twice a week. She never told me what else she had to do, but she seemed to be quite busy. Even though she had a tight schedule, she practiced often and never missed a lesson. We spent each week working on her swing, as well as the rules and etiquette. It seemed that the more she learned about golf as a whole, the more she wanted to play.

We soon came to the end of the series of lessons. At the last lesson I noticed her fun loving smile, that I had learned to look forward to, had disappeared. Now, I know that I always try and make sure my students are having fun while they learn, but that doesn't mean the fun stops because the lessons stop. I asked Shelley how she planned on using her new found golfing abilities, trying to get her to realize this was just the beginning.

"Well, I don't really know. I hadn't really thought past taking the lessons." She said.

"What about Grace who bought the lessons for you? I know she plays golf. Can you ask if she wants to play?" I inquired. If Shelley hadn't planned on actually playing golf, I was a little confused why she would take the lessons in the first place.

"I have lots of friends who take lessons from you and they all enjoy their lessons so much, I just thought it would be fun to take the lessons." As much as I was flattered, it wasn't exactly the best reason to take golf lessons.

"Why don't you get together with some of those women and go play?"

"I'd love to, but I just don't have that kind of time now. I can get away for an hour or so, but that's about it." I really wanted Shelley to get out on the course and play. She had made a great amount of improvement in the last few weeks, but I felt she would really have more fun playing on the course. I didn't want to pry into her personal life, but if she had no intention of playing golf why take the lessons? I know my students and I have fun on the lesson tee, but there are a lot of other ways to have fun, if you aren't planning on playing golf in the future.

Shelley let me know that her husband was dealing with a long term illness, that was taking up much of her time. She had help a few days a week, which she was using to come to the golf course. The golf lesson originally seemed unimportant but what she found was that coming to the golf course was turning into a wonderful break from the intensity of being at home. As great as the break was though, she was limited to how much time she could be gone.

With that information I knew that I wanted to make sure Shelley kept coming to the golf course. That way I knew she would have a least one break each week. Taking care of another person takes a lot of strength and patience. But that strength and patience also needs its own time to be replenished. Leaving the house was giving Shelley added strength for when she was at home.

We devised a plan that would make sure Shelley kept coming to the range. She didn't yet have enough time to even play 9 holes, but that was a goal she was working towards with some extra help at home. We set a time for her to continue to practice each week when I knew I would be at the course. That way she would have someone making sure she didn't just not come.

Through the next few weeks we kept our "date" each week. If I didn't have a lesson, I would grab my own clubs and hit balls while we chatted about golf. I was always careful not to ask about her husband. For the first 6 weeks she never mentioned him and she had her reasons. Most likely because she was coming to the course so she could enjoy herself, while leaving her worries at home.

A few months later, I was sitting in the golf shop finishing up on some paper work when Shelley popped in. "Got a minute?" said a smiling Shelley.

"For you, always. Have a seat."

"I just came by to thank you," she said still standing in the doorway. "You kept me going, when I didn't feel like doing anything." I hadn't seen her this happy for many weeks.

"I had begun to view the world as this dark, disease filled hole. I sometimes wondered why we fight this disease at all. All points where aiming to a horrible ending and I just couldn't handle that." Shelley seemed to almost just be thinking out loud and I was privileged enough to be a part of it.

"When I met you, you just always seem to be happy. It was hard coming to see you and not catch some of your enthusiasm for life," she said.

"Yes" I said, "I have one friend who calls me her personal 'Polly Anna'. Then usually tells me to stop being so annoying!"

We both laughed a little and then Shelley continued, "No matter how bad things were at home, you always seemed to help me find even one good thing going on."

In the golf industry, most of our customers are "mature". Many are retired with a large portion in their late 40's, 50's, 60's and 70's. Due to that fact, I have not only made wonderful friends, but I have also lost quite a few. When I was a seasonal assistant, one of the first things the Head Golf Professional would do upon my return in the spring was to inform me about any of the members who had passed away that winter.

That has taught me that life is short and you need to enjoy it – *right now*. I'm not about to tell people to go out and do crazy things in anticipation of your life ending any time soon. But, enjoying the here and now is a great start.

When I was younger, I remember telling my dad I couldn't wait for some event that was happening in the future. With his wonderful kindness he said, "Don't wish your life away, otherwise one day you'll wake up and it'll be gone." I took what he said that day to heart. Between that comment and the business that I am in, I always try to be thankful for what I have now.

As Shelley left my office that day I was again reminded that golf can bring so much to a person's life. You can't hide from yourself on the golf course. There are good days and bad days. Accept both. The good days are a gift and the bad days show just how special that gift is. Not every day is meant to be perfect, but if you can go away with having learned something about yourself or the game then, even with a perceived "bad score", it's a great day!

With finding the good on our minds, I'd like to discuss what it is that you want from your experience on the course. Let's start by taking a look at some of what golf has to offer. This is a tough section for me to write, because it is hard to put into words, what the experience on the course means.

Golf can teach you so much about yourself. The tricky part, is you have to pay attention - at least a little. As I wrote earlier in the book, you can learn a lot about

136

your playing partners simply by watching how they react to situations on the course. Well, you can use that same technique to learn about yourself. Why do certain shots make us more anxious than others? Why are some seemingly "difficult" shots easier to do sometimes than the "simple" ones?

A few months back, I was about half way through a series of lessons with one of my students. Her swing was improving, but each week she reported that she didn't feel it was translating into a better game on the course. There are times when changes made on the driving range can have a slight delay before they are realized on the course, but I felt like enough time had passed where she should have seen at least some improvement.

We went over in detail how she began each hole, how she approached each shot and what she was focusing on. It all seemed in line with what we were working on at the driving range.

"I guess I'm as good as I'm going to get," she said after we'd gone through her round.

"That is totally not true. You've made some great changes to your swing and we just need to work at getting them to come out on the course," I responded.

As it turned out, Karen played with a group of about 12 ladies, and they rotated who they played with each week. For the past few weeks Karen had been paired with the same woman for 4 rounds.

Karen enjoyed this woman but seemed to think she knew a lot more about golf than she herself did. In Karen's mind, because this woman had been playing longer, she must know more than Karen. This same woman on more than one occasion had told Karen not to "worry" if she didn't get any better, that some people "just aren't cut out for golf." At that point, I took a deep breath realizing what the problem was and that we had a LOT to talk about.

First of all, we are all "cut out for golf". I won't go into why because hopefully you didn't just skip to this point in the book and know what I'm going to say. Second, allowing another person's idea to become your own is not a good idea, especially if they are negative ones. We all have greatness within. Letting it out and believing in your potential – that is the real challenge.

My plan to work through this wasn't to dismiss the experience of whom had said the statement. This in my mind, would be pointless. Every day we have to deflect and block other people's opinions so they don't squash our own vision of ourselves. People are going to say what they want, we need to be able to process the information and either get rid of it or use it to make us better. In golf and in life.

I began by having Karen look at what she was capable of doing when we started the lessons and what she could do now. I then went on to quiz her about how to handle different situations on the course. She answered perfectly. I then asked her, with the abilities she now had, and the knowledge to play effectively, why would she let another person get into her brain and belittle her progress?

She had a lot of self-confidence, when just she and I were talking, but she had trouble expressing it to others. Karen never wanted to appear boastful or rude. Having self confidence in your own abilities isn't being rude, it is all in how you present the information. Deep down Karen didn't agree with this woman, but because she had been taught to be humble she went overboard and internalized the statement.

I explained to her that on the course people are going to say things all the time that might affect your game. Part of learning how to play golf is learning to deflect or ignore those comments. If someone told me that I don't hit the ball very far, (which for a professional woman, I don't) I'd probably laugh. Regardless of how far I hit the ball, I can still break par, so – who cares.

For Karen, we needed to work on having her be more assertive about her own abilities. This didn't necessarily mean she had to go up to this woman and tell her she was crazy, it just meant not having the statement hold any meaning for Karen. Karen needed to ignore the comments and focus on something more positive. When things like that are thrown out there and have the potential to have a negative effect, we need to focus on exactly the opposite. This is where training your brain to think about what you want as opposed to just letting it go, has great value.

I had Karen write down some of the statements that this woman had said to her, then I had her tell me why she felt they were wrong or unjust. It was a great exercise and I could see her strength and happiness improve immediately. I had her practice finding the positive, then we set a plan to meet again and discuss how she was able to use it on the course.

A few weeks passed and as Karen walked up for our lesson, she was beaming she was smiling so bright. "So, I gave a lot of thought to what you said a few weeks ago about not listening to what others say about me. I liked the idea and decided to use this in other areas of my life".

"I did what you had me do for my golf game and dispelled all of what a coworker has been feeding me. I went to my boss earlier this week, telling him how I felt and that I, at the very least deserved a better title than what I had and possibly a small raise."

I couldn't believe what I was hearing. This was a woman who three weeks before would have probably thanked a robber for robbing her. Now, here she was standing in front of me having just challenged her boss. You go girl!

"He agreed with me that they should have made some adjustments earlier. They have already given me the title I wanted and at the end of the month we are going to meet with HR to see about a raise," she smiled.

"That's great, but guess what I'm going to ask next?" I said, with the one-track-golf-pro mind that I have.

"You're going to ask how my golf game is." She answered.

"Yup." I said.

Thankfully, Karen reported that things were going much better. She was able to deflect comments made to her and either laugh them off or simply ignore them. She did admit that it took some time to redirect her thinking. It is a learned habit like everything else, which just take time and practice.

In Karen's case, not having a confrontation was important due to her nature. You may feel differently. Sometimes a simple direct conversation is enough to get a playing partner to keep their not so wanted comments to themselves. Either way is fine, but ultimately you need to decide what's important.

It would be easier if our playing partners kept their opinions to themselves, but that doesn't always happen. However, you don't need to let those comments matter. Either ignore them or remind yourself that those comments don't matter.

Often the same things that give us challenges off the golf course are the ones that challenge us on the golf course. Learning to take charge of your golf game is a great learning process for taking charge in other areas of your life as well.

Many of the challenges we see on the golf course; how to talk to yourself, how to manage difficult playing partners and how to manage our surroundings, are all attributes you have to tackle off the course as well. By learning how to deal with these situations on the course you can be more confident about handling them off the course as well.

Golf is a Life Long Sport

The mental aspect of the game cannot be underplayed. I believe its significance is one of the reasons golfers tend to improve with age. As people mature, they are more comfortable with their abilities and know how to mentally maneuver themselves in the midst of difficult situations. While an 18-year old may be able to blast the ball a great distance, they often lack the mental focus which is an entirely different skill set that may not be fully developed. That mental aspect is essential to success in the sport.

When I was transitioning from a junior membership to an adult one at the club on which I grew up playing, I was allowed to start playing with the Ladies' Club. At first, I thought I'd be able to beat most of the women easily, since I was younger, I was playing golf daily and worked with a coach. But I quickly found myself quite frustrated. At the time, I could hit the ball 250 -270 yards, while most of the ladies hit between 120 to150 yards. I would hit my shot, and excitedly watch the balls sail high into the air and fly beautifully down the fairway. They would hit theirs, often only getting 20 or 30 feet off the ground and sometimes taking two shots to my one. But then we'd meet on the green. I'd sink my two puts and shoot a five. The ladies would all sink their one puts and what did they shoot? Also a five. What? How could that be? I could not understand how we could have such different approaches, or talent, but end with the same result, a five. What I was learning is that there is more than one way to make par!

At the next hole, I'd shoot a four, and the ladies? You guessed it − a four! This was more than a little aggravating from my point of view. My shots flew high into the sky and landed nicely on the green, while their shots never seemed to leave the ground more than 10 feet.

While I had power, they definitely had the accuracy and wisdom I lacked. Among the lessons I learned were not to judge a player by their ball flight, and never to underestimate another player's ability, regardless of what they look like. I was trying to power my way around the golf course, but they were thinking their way around, and doing quite a good job of it. In retrospect, I learned that golf is a sport where age can actually be an advantage!

For many sports, this is just simply not the case. The physical demands on the body are just too great. I realized this early on, and feel it is one of the many assets of golf, allowing it to be a lifelong sport.

Golf is truly a life-long sport, and this knowledge solidified that I could pursue golf as a career and have it be part of my life for as long as I wanted. Age means nothing in golf. We are all equal and can play (thanks to handicaps) against anyone, regardless of age, ability, athleticism, or gender.

For some, the game isn't about playing against an opponent but just being on the golf course. In golf we all have different ideas of what makes our time on the course special. For some the score is irrelevant and it is simply being on the course that is special.

Jerry is a perfect example of this. On a rainy day in early March, I received a phone call from a gentleman inquiring about golf lessons. Jerry explained to me that he was 76 years old and had had a stroke the previous October. We spoke for a few minutes as he asked me a little about my background and how I liked to teach. From our conversation, I assumed he was calling to get his golf game back in shape. But what happened at our first visit wasn't anything I'd expected.

We agreed to meet in the golf shop so I could assess his physical abilities given his recent medical issues, and formulate a plan. As he entered the golf shop, I watched him closely. His physical movement seemed good, even with a cane, which meant that even after having a stroke, golf could continue to be a part of his life. I was excited for him and eager to get him on the range. We sat facing each other, me on the edge of my chair, eager to get started.

I began with my regular questions. I wanted to find out what type of a golfer he had been prior to this stroke, as well as what his expectations were for our lessons. This part of my interview process is important. Sometimes I find my students don't really know what they want. I encourage students to verbalize their goals prior to their first lesson to help pinpoint exactly what it is they hope to achieve. My goal is always to help them go down the right fairway, in order to achieve their goal.

Initially, his answers to my questions seemed a little short and gruff. I assumed he was nervous -- most people don't like to have their golf games analyzed. With some persistence I was able to discover why he had come to see me. His recovery from his stroke was quite significant. He had regained all of his physical mobility, but for his balance. He walked with a cane, to steady himself and prevent himself from falling, he did not use his cane for weight bearing assistance.

He explained to me that due to his lack of balance, he had several falls during his path to recovery. None of his falls resulted in any serious injury, but they caused great, mental anguish for him and his family.

From there, I inquired as to the doctor's prognosis. As it turned out, physically his doctors expected him to be much the same as before the stroke, except for his balance. His arm and leg strength was very good. His balance would improve, but when he was tired it would likely elude him. His doctor's had prescribed some exercises for him to improve his balance, and *walking* was at the top of the list. We walk A LOT in golf. He had been given no limitations on what he could do – only the advice that he should remember that he was 76 and not 16. Fair enough!

I had already begun devising a plan in my head as to how I could assist Jerry with his ability to make, solid consistent contact without falling over. In order to hit the ball any distance there has to be power and contact. The power comes from the length of the swing as well as a persons' strength. Good contact is how close the ball comes to the center of the clubface. I knew we were going to be challenged on the length of the swing so we needed to make sure he hit the ball in the center of the clubface as often as possible. I had to help Jerry think "outside the *tee*-box", and develop a swing that would enable him to continue playing the game, regardless of his balance issues.

In order to keep Jerry balanced, we would need to work on a much shorter back swing and follow through. Making good solid contact was by far more important than club head speed, so shortening the swing was fine. This allowed him to keep his balance, and both feet on the ground, almost every time. (I say almost, because being male, even after a stroke he still just wanted to kill the ball!) We also came up with a plan to get him out on the driving range regularly to practice. It was a very doable plan.

But, I was stopped in my tracks by what happened next.

"So I guess that's it for golf," Jerry said.

I froze. It was like we'd entered a time warp and somehow I had missed an entire conversation. Obviously, my perception of our discussion was quite different from Jerry's. It was then that I noticed that he had not shared my enthusiasm for moving ahead. There was a sadness in Jerry's eyes.

"Jerry, I am a little confused. From what you've told me your balance is really your biggest, and most likely, your only challenge," I said. "We can easily develop a new swing that can account for that. You may not hit the ball as far as you used to, but it beats not playing at all."

Jerry lowered his head. Though I felt I was giving him good news, it seemed to make him even sadder. Clearly, I was missing something. I was beginning to wonder if he liked golf at all, or if someone had put him up to getting a lesson.

I decided to ask more questions. This time I wanted to know about his love for the game, hoping that would give me more information. We talked about where he liked to play, what part of the game he found most rewarding and what he liked best about the game in general. The more he spoke, the more the sparkle returned to his eye. He loved the game, and I could see that not playing had left a vacancy in his life. Now, we were getting somewhere!

But as soon as the conversation returned to the present day, he would return to the demeanor of a child that was told they couldn't have a toy they wanted. His shoulders slumped, his chin lowered and his voice grew softer.

After more probing, the truth finally came out.

"I need you to tell me I'm through, so I can just move on," Jerry said. "My son thinks I need to be at home more, and not running off with this crazy idea of playing golf."

Now, I was starting to get it. He wanted to give up on golf (or at least his son wanted him to), and he wanted someone – me – to give him permission. I wasn't about to do that. He was a perfect contradiction sitting right in front of me. He loved the game, could still physically play, yet he was looking for someone to tell him he couldn't. But the fact that he was sitting in front of me told me he wasn't ready to give up.

"Well," I said, "now that's going to be a problem." I got up, walked over to the golf shop counter and retrieved one of my business cards. Handing it to him, I said, "You will notice that behind my name are three letters. P.G.A. They stand for the Professional Golfers Association of America. With that accreditation, I am committed to growing and developing the game of golf." I couldn't tell at this point if what I was saying was making things better or worse, so I just kept going.

"This is one of the greatest games. It is for EVERYONE. Not just the physically fit. It is for young people, old people, people who are considered to be athletes, and people with no athleticism. We have blind golfers. We have one-armed golfers. I've even seen a gentleman in a wheel chair play the game of golf."

I really wanted to help Jerry, so I had to be brutally honest with him. In a kind, but firm voice I told him, "If all you want me to tell you is to give up golf, well, I'm sorry but I can't do that. I won't do that." As I spoke I noticed that my words didn't upset him, which was a relief. Instead, he lifted his head and focused intently on what I was saying. Even though I had been teaching for many years, I was in unchartered territory. But I knew honesty was the best policy.

"Jerry, I have to ask you something. Why would you think that I, or any other golf professional for that matter would tell you to stop playing golf? From the

149

sound of it, golf would be a great activity for you to KEEP doing."

He sat silently for a moment, turning his cane repeatedly in his hands.

"It's just that, well, my son thinks I'm crazy to want to keep playing this game."

Recognizing that I was involved in some 'family business', I needed to understand more about his relationship with his son if I was going to be able to help him sort through this. It was a place that I was not generally comfortable being, but I couldn't turn back now. This was clearly more than a discussion of Jerry's golf game.

As it turned out, he and his son were quite close. What I took from our conversation was that Jerry is very much a leader and mentor in his family. His stroke was not only hard on himself, but it shook his family to the core. I also learned that Jerry's son had been present for nearly every one of his falls after his stroke. Being close to both my parents, I could only imagine how concerning that would be for his son.

"Jerry," I asked him, "is it just golf that your son wants you to give up?"

He thought for a moment. "No, actually, he doesn't really seem to want me to do much of anything." He paused. "Come to think of it, I can't even get up to get a glass of water without my son jumping up to get it for me."

I asked if it was possible that his son was so shaken by all the events of the previous five months that he just wanted to protect his father. If Jerry didn't do anything, then there was no risk of injury, or worse.

"I guess I never thought of it that way," Jerry replied. He agreed that his son had been very protective of him since his stroke. The falls had only made matters worse.

I continued on. "After listening to you and seeing how much you love the game, I think it would be sad and unnecessary if you gave it up. Golf is such a great game on so many levels: exercise, mentally challenging, and it's a great activity to do with the people you love to be with."

While I can understand where his son was coming from, he also needed to know what his dad really wanted. I had Jerry agree to talk to his son and let him know that golf was a positive part of his life, it fit in with his doctor's orders, and that he wasn't ready to give it up just yet. I assured Jerry that, if need be, I would explain to his son the mechanics and what changes I would make to help ensure a balanced golf swing for Jerry.

Jerry agreed. Once this was finally settled, we both just sat there for a moment. I felt like we had just diffused a live bomb! We then set off for the driving range.

Practice is always important. In Jerry's case practice wasn't just about improving, it was about safety. When he swung too hard or too fast, he lost control of the club and as a result, his balance faltered as well.

After about 20 minutes, Jerry was able, to swing efficiently, using less movement. Sometimes a longer swing is just that – longer. It doesn't necessarily mean better.

Jerry left the lesson with a smile and a plan. Incidentally, he also left with a skip in his step versus a hitch in his heart. Jerry reminded me of the significance of the interconnectedness between one's golf game and one's emotional state.

Over the next few weeks, Jerry persistently kept a regular schedule to come out and practice his new swing with my guidance. He never stayed for very long, but that wasn't so important – just getting *to* the course was. Practice itself is more important to be done often than for long periods of time. Your body will adjust more quickly if you work in small amounts more often than practicing for long periods with long intervals in between. On a few occasions, he brought his son with him. I noticed that on those days, he hit fewer balls, but they did a lot of talking.

Several weeks later, Jerry's son came into the golf shop and asked to speak to me. At first, he asked questions about his dad's swing. He said he was surprised how far his dad was able to hit the ball with his modified swing. But I got the impression that he wasn't here to just talk about his dad's golf swing because he was aimlessly looking around the golf shop as he spoke to me, so I suggested we sit down in my office.

"I don't really want to take up too much of your time," he said, "but I just wanted to say thank you. I haven't seen Dad this happy in a long time. At first I thought he was crazy to want to start playing again, but seeing him out here … he is just so happy." Even though I knew he was truly glad that his Dad was happy, I detected a sadness in his voice.

I tried to reassure him that golf would be something great not only for his Dad, but for both of them to do *together*. I couldn't help but think of my own dad. He had passed away a few years earlier, and I would give anything to have just one more round of golf with him.

"Matt, I understand what you are going through. My dad also had a serious illness. It was one of the hardest things for me to endure. Through my Dad's illness, I learned that even though I wanted to protect him, it was his life, to do with as he chose. The best thing I could do was be there for him. There's nothing wrong with expressing how you feel, but then it's up to them." I reminded Matt that his dad was still very much with him. We can get so worried about what *might* happen to our loved ones that we forget to enjoy what *is* happening. Jerry and his son had a special relationship, and I tried to gently convey that the time they had together might be better spent enjoying the here and now.

At this point, Jerry popped his head into my office. "You two done solving all the world's problems?" I wasn't sure how long he had been standing there, but it didn't really matter. He and his son left that day laughing and joking. I think I even heard some jostling about who had hit the ball the farthest – ah, boys!

Jerry is a perfect example of how anyone can play golf. If you think you can't play because you are too old, too young, too heavy, too thin, or too much of anything else, I'll bet you're wrong. The game of golf can be adjusted to fit each person's individual needs through all stages of life, rather than trying to adjust the person to fit the game. That's one of the great beauties of the sport! Jerry's experience is a great example of overcoming both the physical and mental challenges of the game of golf.

Many older men, like Jerry, find golf to be the perfect outlet for the stresses of daily life. While males, on the whole, tend to enjoy the competitive nature of sports, they find that, as they age, they are unable to compete at the level they once could in contact sports like football, basketball, and soccer. Golf, they discover, allows them the opportunity to keep their competitive spirit alive while protecting their aging bodies (though I did once witness a man break his leg walking off a tee box). Golf provides them "man time" with friends, as well as a good physical and mental challenge, with little impact to their bodies (though they occasionally leave the course with a bruised ego).

I was recently reminded of the life-long nature of golf at an event at my daughter's school. I had the privilege of attending a meeting where Coach Bruce Brown spoke to a group of parents about kids and sports. One statement he made struck me in particular as both a parent and a golf instructor. "By age 18," he began, "most kids, except for exceptional individuals, stop playing any kind of competitive/organized sports." No competitive sports after age 18! The reasons were understandable and all too familiar for many of us: Limited time, increased demands of school, work and life, older bodies that can no longer handle contact sports like football or basketball, or even lower impact sports like track or volleyball, which can still be physically demanding.

But, golf is different. While many kids play high school sports, football, basketball, volleyball or soccer, very few kids have the ability to play at the college level, and even fewer make it to the professional level. Golf is almost the complete reverse. Few kids play golf in high school, some pick it up during college, but most begin after they are more settled in their adult lives. With people like Tiger Woods on the scene, golf has become even more appealing to younger crowds.

The overall appeal of golf has changed tremendously since the sport began centuries ago. While it was once known as a "men only" game, it is now enjoyed equally by males and females of all ages. Even young children love golf. It is a perfect sport for both athletic and non-athletic kids alike, and is in fact a sport that many can excel at, regardless of athleticism. It is not uncommon to see the star basketball player take second position on the high school golf team to a member of the chess club. Remember, golf takes physical ability *and* mental fortitude.

Golf's greater appeal in recent years is also due to some changes in public perception. In years past, the common thinking was that golf, at least in the United States, was only for the wealthy. Playing golf required having the ability to afford a pricey membership at a private club. Today, public and municipal courses far outnumber private golf courses. Growth in the sport has occurred not only due to more available courses, but also, believe it or not, cost. A round at many municipal courses will cost you less than, say, a day on the slopes. A green fee at a local course might run about $28, while a lift ticket can carry a sticker price of $50-75.

Another changing perception is that golf is dad's private outing. Today, more and more kids are learning to play golf. It was once taboo for kids to be in the clubhouse, much less on the golf course. But in recent years, the PGA in particular has realized that getting kids involved is critical to the future success of the game. Golf courses now have more and more programs specifically designed for kids. There are many organizations, most notably The First Tee, devoted specifically to teaching kids about golf.

But young golfers aren't the only ones finding their way onto the course... even Mom is picking up the clubs so the entire family can play together. With increases in gym memberships and fitness classes, we have also seen an increase in female golfers. Women constitute the largest growing market in golf. This may in part be due to men inviting their girlfriends and wives to join them on the course. Men who care not only about their physical and mental health, but also the health of their relationships find that introducing their wives and girlfriends to golf can be beneficial. Once their significant others develop a love for the game, playing a round no longer carriers any guilt about missing "together time"; it can now be spent on the course! When mom, dad, *and* the kids are playing, bringing those clubs along on the family vacation no longer spurns looks of scorn. Win – win!

Regardless of age, we can enjoy playing golf. It is a wonderful way for kids to learn about discipline and etiquette. It is a great way to keep active and social in retirement. From young to old, golf is a *fun* way to enjoy your day.

Made in the USA
Lexington, KY
14 April 2017